The Ave Treasury of
*Catholic Prayers*

"This is a comprehensive collection of prayers that includes traditional and diverse voices. It is an excellent resource for the youth and young adults I minister to and anyone wishing to enhance their prayer lives. I especially love that I could find prayers from Sr. Thea Bowman here!"

**Ogechi Akalegbere**
Catholic speaker and youth and young adult minister

"Just as St. Paul called the early disciples to 'rejoice in your hope, be patient in tribulation, be constant in prayer' (Rm 12:12), we are called now to steep ourselves in hope, patience, and prayer as we walk with the Lord. This wonderful collection of prayers—many familiar to us, others new—will draw us ever closer to the God who made and saved us. Let's join in prayer as together we build the kingdom among us."

**Fr. William Lies, CSC**
Provincial Superior
Congregation of Holy Cross, United States Province of Priests and Brothers

"Human life has different seasons, and each season calls for a specific prayer. This book is a treasure trove that contains valuable prayers for each season of life. Every family needs a copy of this book that is rooted in our rich Catholic spiritual tradition."

**Fr. Fred Jenga, CSC**
President of Holy Cross Family Ministries

"We know we need to draw near to God through prayer, but we don't always have the words to do so. This companion book is perfect to keep with you at all times so that a prayer is never far from your lips."

**Erica Tighe Campbell**
Founder of Be A Heart

"*The Ave Treasury of Catholic Prayers* gathers an especially valuable trove of spiritual treasures drawn from both scripture and tradition. As believers search out the words by which to praise or implore the Lord, these pages come to their ready assistance. Believers will find a faithful, reliable, and time-tested pathway to deeper communion with God."

**Fr. John Burns**
Author of *Lift Up Your Heart*

# The Ave Treasury of
# *Catholic Prayers*

Ave Maria Press  AVE  Notre Dame, Indiana

*Nihil Obstat*: Reverend Monsignor Michael Heintz, PhD
*Censor Librorum*
*Imprimatur*: Most Reverend Kevin C. Rhoades
Bishop of Fort Wayne–South Bend
Given at Fort Wayne, Indiana, on 24 April 2023

Scripture quotations are from the *Revised Standard Version of the Bible—Second Catholic Edition (Ignatius Edition)*, copyright © 2006 National Council of the Churches of Christ in the United States of America. Used by permission. All rights reserved.

The English translation of Antiphons from *The Liturgy of the Hours* © 1973, 1974, 1975, International Commission on English in the Liturgy Corporation (ICEL); excerpts from the English translation of *Order of Christian Funerals* © 1985, 1989, ICEL; excerpts from the English translation of *Book of Blessings* © 1987, ICEL; excerpts from the English translation of *The Roman Missal* © 2010, ICEL. All rights reserved.

Acknowledgments are continued on page 221.

The publisher wishes to thank Martina Bohnslav for her contribution to the arrangement of prayers in this book.

© 2023 by Ave Maria Press, Inc.

All rights reserved. No part of this book may be used or reproduced in any manner whatsoever, except in the case of reprints in the context of reviews, without written permission from Ave Maria Press®, Inc., P.O. Box 428, Notre Dame, IN 46556.

Founded in 1865, Ave Maria Press is a ministry of the Indiana Province of Holy Cross.

www.avemariapress.com

Paperback: ISBN-13 978-1-64680-226-5

E-book: ISBN-13 978-1-64680-227-2

Cover image © GettyImages.com.

Cover and text design by Brianna Dombo.

Printed and bound in the United States of America.

*Library of Congress Cataloging-in-Publication Data is available.*

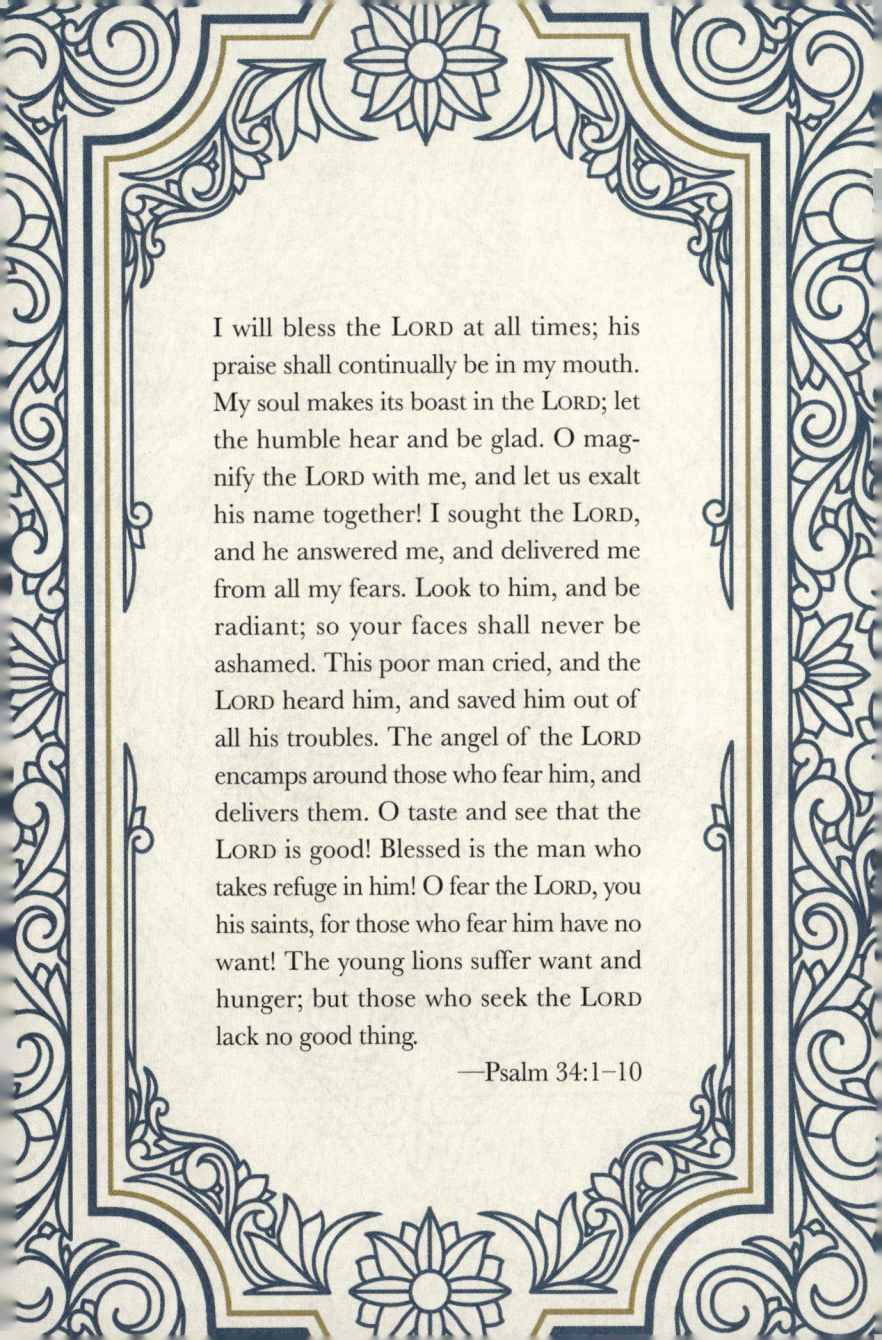

I will bless the Lord at all times; his praise shall continually be in my mouth. My soul makes its boast in the Lord; let the humble hear and be glad. O magnify the Lord with me, and let us exalt his name together! I sought the Lord, and he answered me, and delivered me from all my fears. Look to him, and be radiant; so your faces shall never be ashamed. This poor man cried, and the Lord heard him, and saved him out of all his troubles. The angel of the Lord encamps around those who fear him, and delivers them. O taste and see that the Lord is good! Blessed is the man who takes refuge in him! O fear the Lord, you his saints, for those who fear him have no want! The young lions suffer want and hunger; but those who seek the Lord lack no good thing.

—Psalm 34:1–10

# Contents

| | |
|---|---|
| Introduction | xi |
| General Prayers | 1 |
| Daily Prayers for Speaking with God throughout the Day | 29 |
| Prayers for the Sacrament of Reconciliation | 49 |
| Prayers for the Holy Eucharist | 61 |
| Prayers for Adoration of the Blessed Sacrament | 69 |
| Prayers and Devotions to Jesus Christ | 79 |
| Prayers and Devotions to the Blessed Virgin Mary | 95 |
| Prayers and Devotions to St. Joseph | 117 |
| Prayers of Blessing | 131 |
| Petitionary Prayers: Drawing Close to the Lord in Times of Need | 153 |
| Prayers for Deliverance | 161 |
| Prayers for Special Graces | 165 |
| Prayers of Surrender to God's Loving Will | 179 |
| Prayers for the Grace of Forgiveness | 183 |
| Intercessory Prayers | 187 |
| Prayers of Thanksgiving and Praise | 217 |
| Acknowledgments | 221 |
| Index | 227 |

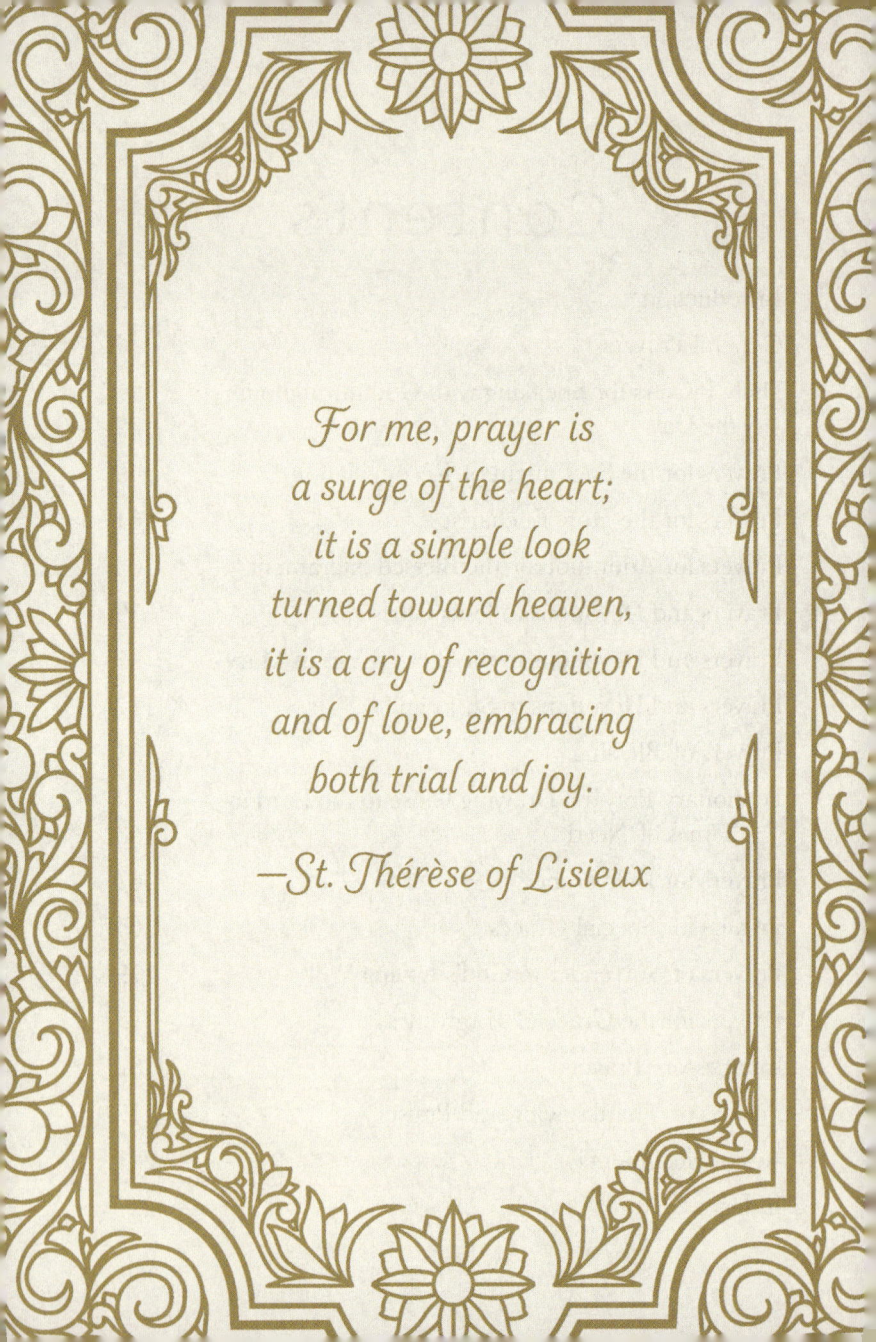

*For me, prayer is
a surge of the heart;
it is a simple look
turned toward heaven,
it is a cry of recognition
and of love, embracing
both trial and joy.*

—St. Thérèse of Lisieux

# Introduction

> Our thoughts are not easily God's thoughts, nor our wills His will. But as we listen to Him and converse with Him, our minds will be given to understand Him and His designs. ... We pray with the church, we pray in community and we pray in solitude. Prayer is our faith attending to the Lord, and in that faith we meet him individually, yet we also stand in the company of others who know God as their Father.
>
> —Constitutions of the Congregation of Holy Cross, no. 3.22–23

Whether you learned to pray the Rosary as a child or are relatively new to the faith, your soul will flourish as you engage in a lifelong dialogue with God, praying both "in solitude" and "in community." Outside the liturgy, we also pray truly in community through the Communion of Saints, the "cloud of witnesses" referenced in the first two verses of Hebrews 12, who surround us day and night, interceding on our behalf.

This book was created to enrich your ongoing dialogue with God, as well as with Mary and the saints. Drawn from the deep well of our faith tradition, these prayers are passed to us from the Church to sustain and encourage us—especially when we have intentions that are so important to us that we struggle to find the words to express them adequately to God. We hope that these time-tested prayers from the treasury of our faith will be a source of inspiration, reflection, and reassurance.

This exquisite collection of prayers—150 of them—has been carefully curated to represent the truly "catholic" nature of the Church, with prayers from every corner of the world and from throughout her history. Slip this book into your pocket or handbag to refer to throughout the day. Let it guide you in praying not only the prayers you ought to know (General Prayers) but also the prayers you need, when you need them most. You will find, too, a scattering of quotes from the saints—each a role model of personal prayer—to inspire you to offer up your own intentions. (If you would like a place to write these down, as a record of your own prayer journey, pick up a copy of *The Ave Prayer Intentions Journal*.)

This prayer book offers not only prayers you can raise to God throughout the day but also prayers of adoration and blessing, contrition, thanksgiving and praise, and supplication to meet the need of the moment. It also contains special devotional prayers to Jesus, Mary, and Joseph, as well as prayers you can offer before and after receiving the sacraments or at eucharistic adoration. Whatever grace you need in the moment, there is a suitable prayer to give voice to the deepest and most pressing intentions of your heart. Whether you work your way through the book from the first page to the last, or flip through and commit to memory a few favorites, this prayer book is one you will find yourself turning to again and again, settling in quietly to hear the voice of God as these prayers help you find the words you most want to say to the Lord, who is waiting to hear from you.

> *Do not seek to have your trials lifted from you. Instead, ask for the grace to bear them well.*
>
> —St. Andrè Bessette

# General Prayers

Lord, teach me how to pray. O Lord, in my meditation let a fire flame out. Open my lips, O Lord, and my mouth will declare Your praise.

—St. John Berchmans

| | | |
|---|---|---|
| 1. | The Sign of the Cross | 3 |
| 2. | The Our Father (The Lord's Prayer) | 3 |
| 3. | Hail Mary | 4 |
| 4. | Glory Be | 4 |
| 5. | O My Jesus Prayer | 5 |
| 6. | The Jesus Prayer | 5 |
| 7. | Te Deum | 6 |
| 8. | Veni Sancte Spiritus (Come, Holy Spirit) | 9 |
| 9. | The Apostles' Creed | 11 |
| 10. | The Nicene Creed | 12 |

| | | |
|---|---|---|
| 11. | Confiteor | 14 |
| 12. | Act of Spiritual Communion— | |
| | St. Alphonsus Liguori | 15 |
| 13. | Act of Faith | 16 |
| 14. | Act of Hope | 16 |
| 15. | Act of Charity | 17 |
| 16. | Prayer for the Faithful Departed | 17 |
| 17. | Angel of God | 18 |
| 18. | Litany of Saints | 19 |
| 19. | Prayer to the Holy Family—Pope Francis | 26 |

## The Sign of the Cross

In the name of the Father,
and of the Son,
and of the Holy Spirit.
Amen.


## The Our Father
## (The Lord's Prayer)

Our Father, who art in heaven,
hallowed be thy name;
thy kingdom come,
thy will be done
on earth as it is in heaven.
Give us this day our daily bread,
and forgive us our trespasses,
as we forgive those who trespass against us;
and lead us not into temptation,
but deliver us from evil.
Amen.

## Hail Mary

Hail Mary, full of grace,
the Lord is with you.
Blessed are you among women,
and blessed is the fruit of your womb, Jesus.
Holy Mary, Mother of God, pray for us
 sinners,
now and at the hour of our death. Amen.

## Glory Be

Glory be to the Father,
and to the Son,
and to the Holy Spirit.
As it was in the beginning,
is now,
and ever shall be,
world without end.
Amen.

## O My Jesus Prayer

O my Jesus,
forgive us our sins,
save us from the fires of hell,
and lead all souls to heaven,
especially those most in need of thy mercy.
Amen.


## The Jesus Prayer

Lord, have mercy on me a sinner.

# Te Deum

You are God: we praise you;
You are the Lord: we acclaim you;
You are the eternal Father:
All creation worships you.

To you all angels, all the powers of heaven,
Cherubim and Seraphim, sing in endless praise:
Holy, holy, holy Lord, God of power and might,
heaven and earth are full of your glory.

The glorious company of apostles praise you.
The noble fellowship of prophets praise you.
The white-robed army of martyrs praise you.

Throughout the world the holy Church acclaims you:
Father, of majesty unbounded,
your true and only Son, worthy of all worship,
and the Holy Spirit, advocate and guide.

You, Christ, are the king of glory,
the eternal Son of the Father.
When you became man to set us free
you did not spurn the Virgin's womb.

You overcame the sting of death,
and opened the kingdom of heaven to all believers.
You are seated at God's right hand in glory.
We believe that you will come, and be our judge.

Come then, Lord, and help your people,
bought with the price of your own blood,
and bring us with your saints
to glory everlasting.

Save your people, Lord, and bless your inheritance.
R. Govern and uphold them now and always.
Day by day we bless you.
R. We praise your name forever.
Keep us today, Lord, from all sin.
R. Have mercy on us, Lord, have mercy.
Lord, show us your love and mercy;
R. For we put our trust in you.

In you, Lord, is our hope:
R. And we shall never hope in vain.

# *Veni Sancte Spiritus*
## *(Come, Holy Spirit)*

Come, Holy Spirit, come!
And from your celestial home
Shed a ray of light divine!

Come, Father of the poor!
Come, source of all our store!
Come, within our bosoms shine!

You, of comforters the best;
You, the soul's most welcome guest;
Sweet refreshments here below;

In our labor, rest most sweet;
Grateful coolness in the heat;
Solace in the midst of woe.

O most blessed Light divine,
Shine within these hearts of yours,
And our inmost being fill!

Where you are not, man has naught,
Nothing good in deed or thought,
Nothing free from taint or ill.

Heal our wounds, our strength renew;
On our dryness pour your dew;
Wash the stains of guilt away;

Bend the stubborn heart and will;
Melt the frozen, warm the chill;
Guide the steps that go astray.

On our faithful, who adore
And confess you, evermore
In your sev'nold gift descend;

Give them virtue's sure reward;
Give them your salvation, Lord;
Give them joys that never end. Amen.
Alleluia.

# The Apostles' Creed

I believe in God, the Father almighty,
creator of heaven and earth.
I believe in Jesus Christ, his only Son, our Lord.
He was conceived by the power of the Holy Spirit
and born of the Virgin Mary.
He suffered under Pontius Pilate,
was crucified, died, and was buried.
He descended to the dead.
On the third day he rose again.
He ascended into heaven,
and is seated at the right hand of the Father.
He will come again to judge the living and the dead.
I believe in the Holy Spirit,
the holy Catholic Church,
the communion of saints,
the forgiveness of sins,
the resurrection of the body,
and life everlasting. Amen.

# The Nicene Creed

I believe in one God,
the Father almighty,
maker of heaven and earth,
of all things visible and invisible.
I believe in one Lord, Jesus Christ,
the Only Begotten Son of God,
born of the Father before all ages.
God from God, Light from Light,
true God from true God,
begotten, not made, consubstantial with the
 Father;
through him all things were made.
For us men and for our salvation
he came down from heaven,
and by the Holy Spirit was incarnate of the
 Virgin Mary,
and became man.
(*making a profound bow*)
For our sake he was crucified under Pontius
 Pilate,
he suffered death and was buried,
and rose again on the third day
in accordance with the Scriptures.
He ascended into heaven
and is seated at the right hand of the Father.

He will come again in glory
to judge the living and the dead,
and his kingdom will have no end.
I believe in the Holy Spirit, the Lord, the giver of life,
who proceeds from the Father and the Son,
who with the Father and the Son is adored and glorified,
who has spoken through the prophets.
I believe in one, holy, catholic, and apostolic Church.
I confess one Baptism for the forgiveness of sins,
and I look forward to the resurrection of the dead
and the life of the world to come. Amen.

## *Confiteor*

I confess to almighty God
and to you, my brothers and sisters,
that I have greatly sinned,
in my thoughts and in my words,
in what I have done and in what I have failed
    to do,
(*striking the breast*)
through my fault, through my fault,
through my most grievous fault;
therefore I ask blessed Mary, ever-Virgin,
all the angels and saints,
and you, my brothers and sisters,
to pray for me to the Lord our God.

# Act of Spiritual Communion

My Jesus, I believe that you are present in the most Blessed Sacrament. I love You above all things and I desire to receive You into my soul. Since I cannot now receive You sacramentally, come at least spiritually into my heart. I embrace You as if You were already there, and unite myself wholly to You. Never permit me to be separated from You. Amen.

St. Alphonsus Liguori

## Act of Faith

O my God! I firmly believe all the sacred truths, which Thy Holy Catholic Church believes and teaches; because Thou hast revealed them, who canst neither deceive, nor be deceived.

## Act of Hope

O my God! Relying on Thy infinite goodness and promises, I hope to obtain the pardon of my sins, the assistance of Thy grace, and life everlasting; through the merits of Jesus Christ, my Lord, and redeemer.

## Act of Charity

O my God! I love Thee above all things with my whole heart and soul, because Thou art infinitely amiable and deserving of all love. I love also my neighbor as myself for the love of Thee. I forgive all who have injured me, and ask pardon of all whom I have injured.

## Prayer for the Faithful Departed

Eternal rest grant unto them, O Lord.
R. And let the perpetual light shine upon them. And may the souls of all the faithful departed, through the mercy of God, rest in peace. Amen.

## Angel of God

O angel of God, to whose holy care I am committed by the supreme clemency, enlighten, defend, and protect me this night from all sin and danger. Amen.

# Litany of Saints

Lord, have mercy on us.
*Christ, have mercy on us.*
Lord, have mercy on us. Christ hear us.
*Christ, graciously hear us.*
God, the Father of heaven, *have mercy on us.*
God, the Son, Redeemer of the world, *have mercy on us.*
God, the Holy Ghost, *have mercy on us.*
Holy Trinity, one God, *have mercy on us.*
Holy Mary, *pray for us.*
Holy Mother of God, *pray for us.*
Holy Virgin of virgins, *pray for us.*
St. Michael, *pray for us.*
St. Gabriel, *pray for us.*
St. Raphael, *pray for us.*
All you holy angels and archangels, *pray for us.*
All you holy Orders of blessed Spirits, *pray for us.*
St. John the Baptist, *pray for us.*
St. Joseph, *pray for us.*
All you holy Patriarchs and Prophets, *pray for us.*
St. Peter, *pray for us.*
St. Paul, *pray for us.*
St. Andrew, *pray for us.*

St. James, *pray for us.*
St. John, *pray for us.*
St. Thomas, *pray for us.*
St. James, *pray for us.*
St. Philip, *pray for us.*
St. Bartholomew, *pray for us.*
St. Matthew, *pray for us.*
St. Simon, *pray for us.*
St. Thaddeus, *pray for us.*
St. Matthias, *pray for us.*
St. Barnabas, *pray for us.*
St. Luke, *pray for us.*
St. Mark, *pray for us.*
All you holy apostles and evangelists, *pray for us.*
All you holy disciples of our Lord, *pray for us.*
All you holy Innocents, *pray for us.*
St. Stephen, *pray for us.*
St. Laurence, *pray for us.*
St. Vincent, *pray for us.*
St. Fabian and St. Sebastian, *pray for us.*
St. John and St. Paul, *pray for us.*
St. Cosmas and St. Damian, *pray for us.*
St. Gervase and St. Protase, *pray for us.*
All you holy Martyrs, *pray for us.*
St. Sylvester, *pray for us.*
St. Gregory, *pray for us.*
St. Ambrose, *pray for us.*

St. Augustine, *pray for us.*
St. Jerome, *pray for us.*
St. Martin, *pray for us.*
St. Nicholas, *pray for us.*
All you holy bishops and confessors, *pray for us.*
All you holy Doctors, *pray for us.*
St. Anthony, *pray for us.*
St. Benedict, *pray for us.*
St. Bernard, *pray for us.*
St. Dominic, *pray for us.*
St. Francis, *pray for us.*
All you holy priests and Levites, *pray for us.*
All you holy monks and hermits, *pray for us.*
St. Mary Magdalen, *pray for us.*
St. Agatha, *pray for us.*
St. Lucy, *pray for us.*
St. Agnes, *pray for us.*
St. Cecilia, *pray for us.*
St. Catherine, *pray for us.*
St. Anastasia, *pray for us.*
All you holy virgins and widows, *pray for us.*
All you holy men and women, Saints of God, *make intercession for us.*
Be merciful unto us.
*Graciously hear us, O Lord.*
From all evil,

*O Lord, deliver us.*
From all sin,
*O Lord, deliver us.*
From thy wrath,
*O Lord, deliver us.*
From a sudden and unprovided death,
*O Lord, deliver us.*
From the deceits of the devil,
*O Lord, deliver us.*
From anger, hatred, and all ill will,
*O Lord, deliver us.*
From the spirit of fornication,
*O Lord, deliver us.*
From lightning and tempest,
*O Lord, deliver us.*
From everlasting death,
*O Lord, deliver us.*
Through the mystery of thy holy Incarnation,
*O Lord, deliver us.*
Through thy Coming,
*O Lord, deliver us.*
Through thy Nativity,
*O Lord, deliver us.*
Through thy Baptism and holy Fasting,
*O Lord, deliver us.*
Through thy Cross and Passion,

*O Lord, deliver us.*
Through thy Death and Burial,
*O Lord, deliver us.*
Through thy holy Resurrection,
*O Lord, deliver us.*
Through thy admirable Ascension,
*O Lord, deliver us.*
Through the coming of the Holy Ghost, the Paraclete,
*O Lord, deliver us.*
In the day of judgment,
*O Lord, deliver us.*
We sinners,
*We beseech thee, hear us.*
That thou spare us,
*We beseech thee, hear us.*
That thou pardon us,
*We beseech thee, hear us.*
That thou vouchsafe to bring us to true penance,
*We beseech thee, hear us.*
That thou vouchsafe to govern and preserve thy holy Church,
*We beseech thee, hear us.*
That thou vouchsafe to preserve our Apostolic Prelate and all ecclesiastical orders in thy holy religion,

*We beseech thee, hear us.*

That thou vouchsafe to humble the enemies of thy holy Church,

*We beseech thee, hear us.*

That thou vouchsafe to give peace and true concord to Christian kings and princes,

*We beseech thee, hear us.*

That thou vouchsafe to grant peace and unity to all Christian people,

*We beseech thee, hear us.*

That thou vouchsafe to confirm and preserve us in thy holy service,

*We beseech thee, hear us.*

That thou lift up our minds to heavenly desires,

*We beseech thee, hear us.*

That thou render eternal good things to all our benefactors,

*We beseech thee, hear us.*

That thou deliver our souls, and those of our brethren, kinsfolk, and benefactors, from eternal damnation,

*We beseech thee, hear us.*

That thou vouchsafe to give and preserve the fruits of the earth,

*We beseech thee, hear us.*

That thou vouchsafe to give eternal rest to all the faithful departed,
*We beseech thee, hear us.*
That thou vouchsafe to graciously to hear us,
*We beseech thee, hear us.*
Son of God,
*We beseech thee, hear us.*
Lamb of God, who takest away the sins of the world,
*Spare us, O Lord.*
Lamb of God, who takest away the sins of the world,
*Here us, O Lord.*
Lamb of God, who takest away the sins of the world, *have mercy on us.*
Christ, hear us;
*Christ, graciously hear us.*
Lord, have mercy on us;
*Christ, have mercy on us.*
Lord, have mercy on us;
*Christ, have mercy on us.*
Lord, have mercy on us.
*Our Father . . .*
And lead us not into temptation.
*But deliver us from evil. Amen.*

# Prayer to the Holy Family

Jesus, Mary and Joseph, in you we contemplate the splendor of true love; to you we turn with trust. Holy Family of Nazareth, grant that our families too may be places of communion and prayer, authentic schools of the Gospel and small domestic churches. Holy Family of Nazareth, may families never again experience violence, rejection, and division; may all who have been hurt or scandalized find ready comfort and healing. Holy Family of Nazareth, make us once more mindful of the sacredness and inviolability of the family, and its beauty in God's plan. Jesus, Mary, and Joseph, graciously hear our prayer. Amen.

Pope Francis

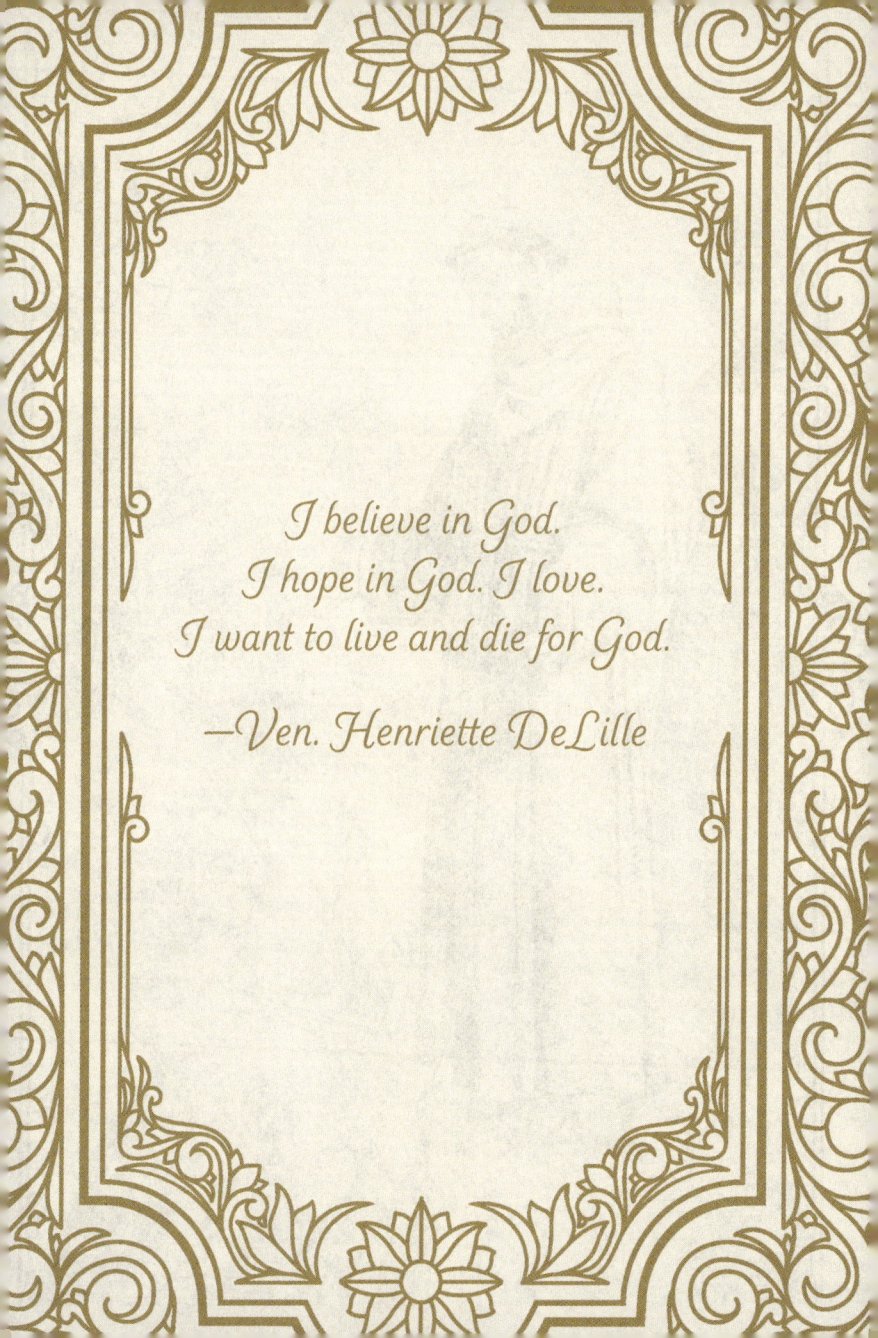

*I believe in God.
I hope in God. I love.
I want to live and die for God.*

—Ven. Henriette DeLille

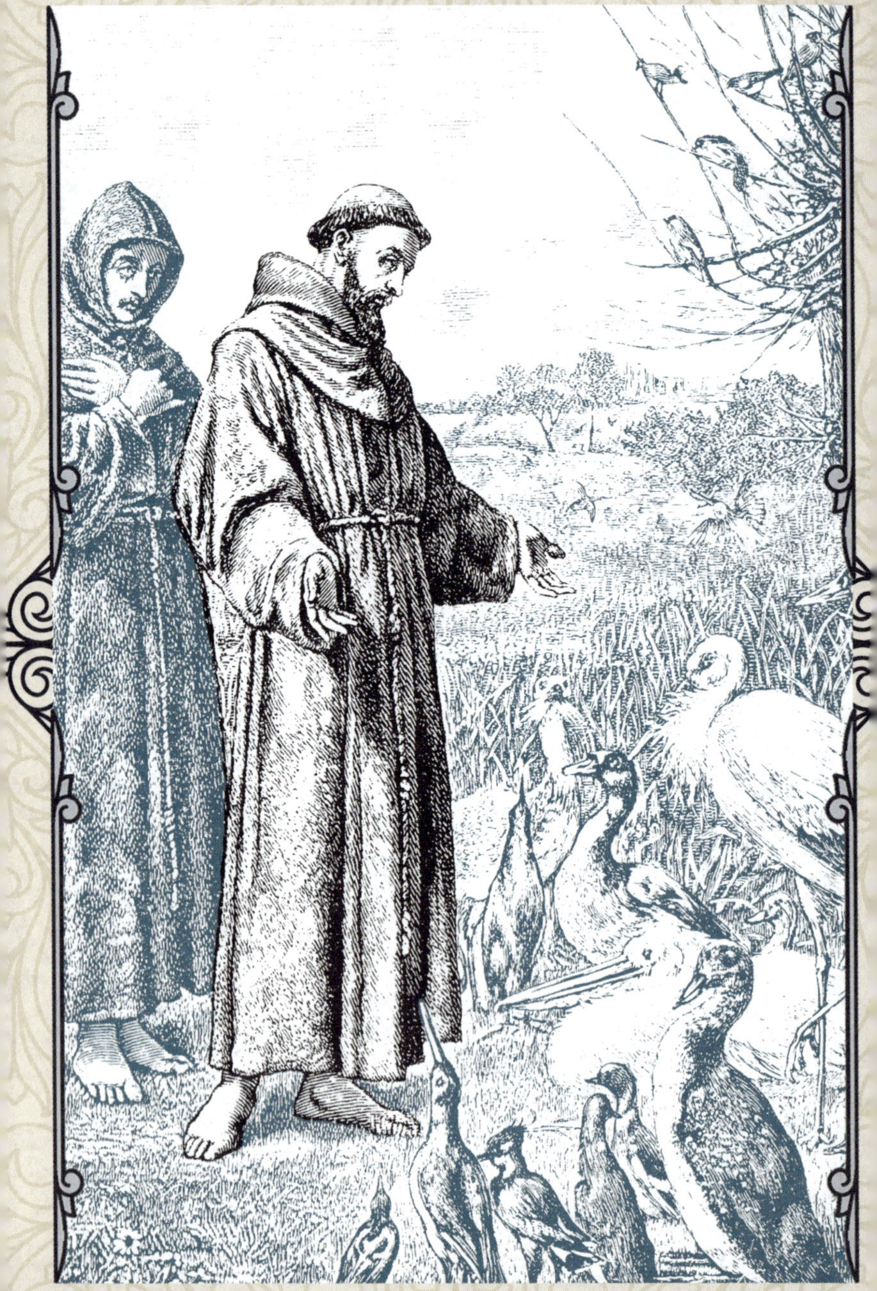

# Daily Prayers for Speaking with God throughout the Day

I am definitely loved, and whatever happens to me, I am awaited by this love. And so, my life is good.

—St. Josephine Bakhita

## *Morning Prayers*

| | | |
|---|---|---|
| 20. | When I Awake—Psalm 17:15 | 32 |
| 21. | I Will Sing—Psalm 59:16 | 32 |
| 22. | A Morning Prayer (Canticle of Zechariah: The Benedictus)—Luke 1:68–79 | 33 |

| | | |
|---|---|---|
| 23. | Morning Offering—<br>Fr. François-Xavier Gautrelet | 34 |
| 24. | My Life Is an Instant—St. Thérèse of Lisieux | 35 |
| 25. | Suscipe Prayer—St. Ignatius of Loyola | 35 |
| 26. | The Eyes of All Look to You—<br>Psalm 145:15–16 | 36 |
| 27. | Blessing before Meals (Bless Us, O Lord) | 36 |
| 28. | Grace after Meals | 37 |
| 29. | Lord, You Have Fed Us | 37 |

## *Prayers before Work*

| | | |
|---|---|---|
| 30. | Actiones Nostras | 38 |
| 31. | Prayer of St. Francis | 39 |

## *Midday Prayers*

| | | |
|---|---|---|
| 32. | The Angelus | 40 |
| 33. | Regina Coeli (Queen of Heaven) | 41 |

## *Afternoon Prayer*

| | | |
|---|---|---|
| 34. | Three O'clock Prayer | 42 |

## Evening Prayer

| | | |
|---|---|---|
| 35. | An Evening Prayer (Canticle of Mary: The Magnificat)—Luke 1:46–55 | 43 |

## Bedtime Prayers

| | | |
|---|---|---|
| 36. | Night Holds No Terrors for Me | 45 |
| 37. | Watch, O Lord—St. Augustine | 45 |
| 38. | Short Guide to the Examen | 46 |
| 39. | Night Prayer (Canticle of Simeon: The Nunc Dimittis)—Luke 2:29–32 | 47 |
| 40. | Protect Us, Lord | 47 |

## Morning Prayers

### When I Awake

When I awake, I shall be satisfied
 with beholding your form.

Psalm 17:15

### I Will Sing

I will sing aloud of your mercy in the morning.

Psalm 59:16

# A Morning Prayer (Canticle of Zechariah: The Benedictus)

Blessed be the Lord God of Israel,
for he has visited and redeemed his people,
and has raised up a horn of salvation for us
in the house of his servant David,
as he spoke by the mouth of his holy
    prophets from of old,
that we should be saved from our enemies,
and from the hand of all who hate us;
to perform the mercy promised to our
    fathers,
and to remember his holy covenant,
the oath which he swore to our father
    Abraham, to grant us
that we, being delivered from the hand of
    our enemies,
might serve him without fear,
in holiness and righteousness before him all
    the days of our life.
And you, child, will be called the prophet of
    the Most High;
for you will go before the Lord to prepare
    his ways,

to give knowledge of salvation to his people
in the forgiveness of their sins,
through the tender mercy of our God,
when the day shall dawn upon us from on
    high
to give light to those who sit in darkness
and in the shadow of death,
to guide our feet into the way of peace.

                                  Luke 1:68–79

## Morning Offering

O Jesus, through the Immaculate Heart of
    Mary,
I offer you my prayers, works, joys, and sufferings of this day
for all the intentions of your Sacred Heart
in union with the Holy Sacrifice of the Mass
    throughout the world,
for the salvation of souls, the reparation of
    sins, the reunion of all Christians,
and in particular for the intentions of the
    Holy Father this month.
Amen.

                        Fr. François-Xavier Gautrelet

## My Life Is an Instant

My life is an instant,
a fleeting hour.
My life is a moment,
which swiftly escapes me.
O my God, you know that
on earth I have only today
to love you.

St. Thérèse of Lisieux

## Suscipe Prayer

Receive, Lord, all my liberty, my memory, my understanding, and my whole will. You have given me all that I have, all that I am, and I surrender all to your divine will, that you dispose of me. Give me only your love and your grace. With this I am rich enough, and I have no more to ask.

St. Ignatius of Loyola

## The Eyes of All Look to You

The eyes of all look to you
> and you give them their food in due season.

You open your hand,
> you satisfy the desire of every living thing.

*Psalm 145:15–16*

## Blessing before Meals (Bless Us, O Lord)

Bless us, O Lord, and these thy gifts, which we are about to receive from thy bounty; through Christ our Lord. Amen.

## Grace after Meals

We give thee thanks, Almighty God, for these and all thy blessings; through Christ our Lord. Amen.

## Lord, You Have Fed Us

Lord, you have fed us from your gifts and favors; fill us with your mercy, for you live and reign for ever and ever.

## Prayers before Work

### Actiones Nostras

Inspire our actions, Lord, and accompany them with your help, so that our every word and action may always begin and end in you.

# Prayer of St. Francis

Lord, make me an instrument of your peace:
Where there is hatred, let me sow love;
Where there is injury, pardon;
Where there is doubt, faith;
Where there is despair, hope;
Where there is darkness, light;
Where there is sadness, joy.
O divine Master, grant that I may not so much seek
To be consoled as to console,
To be understood as to understand,
To be loved as to love.
For it is in giving that we receive,
It is in pardoning that we are pardoned,
And it is in dying that we are born to eternal life.
Amen.

St. Francis of Assisi

## Midday Prayers

## The Angelus

The Angel of the Lord declared unto Mary,
and she conceived of the Holy Spirit.
Hail Mary . . .

Behold the handmaid of the Lord.
Be it done unto me according to thy word.
Hail Mary . . .

And the Word was made Flesh
and dwelt among us.
Hail Mary . . .

Pray for us, O Holy Mother of God,
that we may be made worthy of the promises
 of Christ.

Let us pray.
Pour forth, we beseech thee, O Lord, thy grace into our hearts; that we to whom the incarnation of Christ, thy Son, was made known by the message of an angel, may by his Passion and Cross be brought to the glory

of his Resurrection, through the same Christ Our Lord.

# Regina Coeli
# (Queen of Heaven)

*This prayer is said at noon during the Easter season.*

Queen of Heaven, rejoice, Alleluia,
for he whom you did merit to bear, Alleluia,
has risen, as he said, Alleluia.
Pray for us to God, Alleluia.
Rejoice and be glad, O Virgin Mary, Alleluia,
for the Lord has truly risen, Alleluia.

Let us pray.
O God, who gave joy to the world through the Resurrection of your Son, our Lord Jesus Christ, grant we beseech you, that through the intercession of the Virgin Mary, his Mother, we may obtain the joys of everlasting life. Through the same Christ our Lord.

*Afternoon Prayer*

## Three O'clock Prayer

You expired, Jesus, but the source of life gushed forth for souls and the ocean of mercy opened up for the whole world. O Fountain of Life, unfathomable Divine Mercy, cover the whole world and empty yourself out upon us. O Blood and Water which gushed forth from the heart of Jesus as a Fountain of Mercy for us, I trust in you.

*Evening Prayer*

# An Evening Prayer (Canticle of Mary: The Magnificat)

And Mary said,
My soul magnifies the Lord,
and my spirit rejoices in God my Savior,
for he has regarded the low estate of his handmaiden.
For behold, henceforth all generations will call me blessed;
for he who is mighty has done great things for me,
and holy is his name.
And his mercy is on those who fear him
from generation to generation.
He has shown strength with his arm,
he has scattered the proud in the imagination of their hearts,
he has put down the mighty from their thrones,
and exalted those of low degree;
he has filled the hungry with good things,

and the rich he has sent empty away.
He has helped his servant Israel,
in remembrance of his mercy,
as he spoke to our fathers,
to Abraham and to his posterity forever.

Luke 1:46–55

## Bedtime Prayers

## Night Holds No Terrors for Me

Night holds no terrors for me, sleeping under God's wings.
In you, my God, my body will rest in hope.

## Watch, O Lord

Watch, O Lord, with those who work or wake or weep tonight.
Give the angels and saints charge over those who sleep.
O Lord Jesus Christ, tend your sick ones,
rest your weary ones,
bless your dying ones,
soothe the suffering ones,
pity all the afflicted ones,
shield the joyful ones,
and all for your love's sake. Amen.

St. Augustine

# Short Guide to the Examen

*An examen is a daily (or twice-daily) **Ignatian** practice that entails placing ourselves in the presence of God and reflecting upon the following:*

- When was God's presence most acutely felt in my life today?
- For what moment (or moments) am I most thankful?
- In what ways have my emotions affected my choices today?
- Can I recall anything I need to forgive or for which I need forgiveness?
- As I anticipate tomorrow, where do I especially need God's presence?

# Night Prayer (Canticle of Simeon: The Nunc Dimittis)

Lord, now you let your servant go in peace;
your word has been fulfilled:
my own eyes have seen the salvation
which you have prepared in the sight of
  every people:
a light to reveal you to the nations
and the glory of your people, Israel.

Luke 2:29–32

# Protect Us, Lord

Protect us, Lord, as we stay awake;
watch over us as we sleep,
that awake, we may keep watch with Christ,
and asleep, rest in his peace.

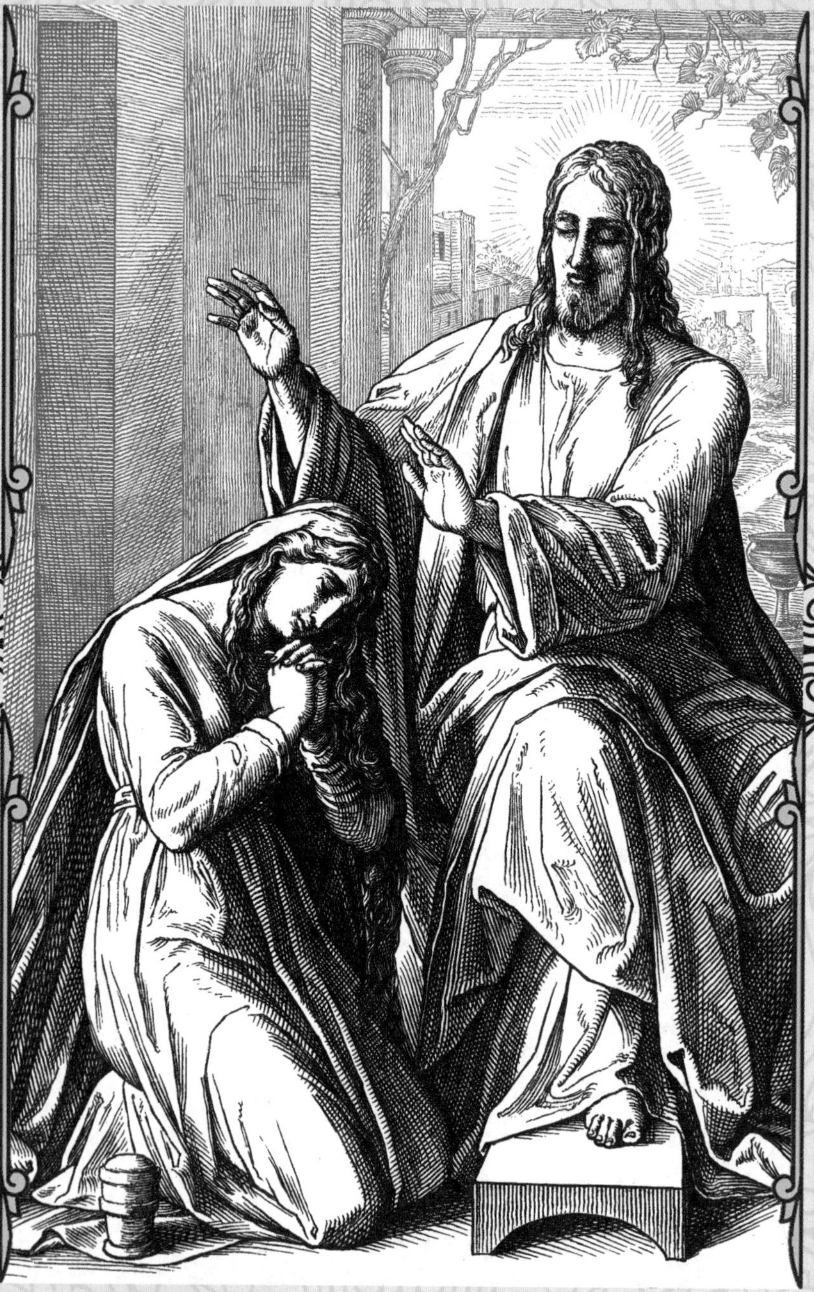

# Prayers for the Sacrament of Reconciliation

Likewise the Spirit helps us in our weakness; for we do not know how to pray as we ought, but the Spirit himself intercedes for us with sighs too deep for words. And he who searches the hearts of men knows what is the mind of the Spirit, because the Spirit intercedes for the saints according to the will of God.
—Romans 8:26–27

| | | |
|---|---|---|
| 41. | Have Mercy on Me, O God—Psalm 51:1–2, 10 | 51 |
| 42. | Prayer before the Examination of Conscience | 51 |
| 43. | Examination of Conscience Based on the Ten Commandments | 53 |

| | | |
|---|---|---|
| 44. | Examination of Conscience Based on the Beatitudes | 56 |
| 45. | Act of Contrition I | 58 |
| 46. | Act of Contrition II—St. Julie Billiart | 58 |
| 47. | Prayer of Heartfelt Penitence and Thanksgiving—Psalm 33:18–22 | 59 |
| 48. | O Lord, You Have Searched—Psalm 139:1 | 59 |

# Have Mercy on Me, O God

Have mercy on me, O God, according to your merciful love; according to your abundant mercy blot out my transgressions. Wash me thoroughly from my iniquity, and cleanse me from my sin! . . . Create in me a clean heart, O God, and put a new and right spirit within me.

Psalm 51:1–2, 10

# Prayer before the Examination of Conscience

O Most Holy Trinity, Father, Son and Holy Spirit, worthy of all my love, I humbly present myself before You. Look upon me with merciful eyes and help me to be reconciled to You by a good Confession. But as I can do nothing if You do not help me, I implore You in Your tender mercy to enlighten me, that I may know all my sins and detest them with my whole heart.

O Jesus, ever flowing fountain of compassion, I approach You to cleanse me from all my sins. O Divine Physician, heal my soul. O infinite Love, enkindle the flames of Your Love in my soul that it may love nothing but You. May this Confession bring about in me an entire change in my life so that I may be fully reconciled to You.

Mother of God, you are so charitable to sinners who desire repentance; assist me to make a good Confession. My Guardian Angel, help me to discover the sins I have committed. My Patron Saint and all you Saints of Heaven, pray for me that I may bring forth worthy fruits of repentance. Amen.

# Examination of Conscience Based on the Ten Commandments

*I am the L̲o̲r̲d̲ your God: you shall not have strange Gods before me.*

> Have I treated people, events, or things as more important than God?

*You shall not take the name of the L̲o̲r̲d̲ your God in vain.*

> Have my words, actively or passively, put down God, the Church, or people?

*Remember to keep holy the L̲o̲r̲d̲'s Day.*

> Do I go to Mass every Sunday (or Saturday Vigil) and on Holy Days of Obligation (January 1; the Ascension; August 15; November 1; December 8; December 25)? Do I avoid, when possible, work that impedes worship to God, joy for the Lord's Day, and proper relaxation of mind and body? Do I look for ways to spend time with family or in service on Sunday?

*Honor your father and your mother.*

> Do I show my parents due respect? Do I seek to maintain good communication with my parents where possible? Do I criticize them for lacking skills I think they should have?

*You shall not kill.*

> Have I harmed another through physical, verbal, or emotional means, including gossip or manipulation of any kind?

*You shall not commit adultery.*

> Have I respected the physical and sexual dignity of others and of myself?

*You shall not steal.*

> Have I taken or wasted time or resources that belonged to another?

*You shall not bear false witness against your neighbor.*

> Have I gossiped, told lies, or embellished stories at the expense of another?

*You shall not covet your neighbor's spouse.*

> Have I honored my spouse with my full affection and exclusive love?

*You shall not covet your neighbor's goods.*

> Am I content with my own means and needs, or do I compare myself to others unnecessarily?

# Examination of Conscience Based on the Beatitudes

*Blessed are the poor in spirit, for theirs is the kingdom of heaven.*

> Do I live in a spirit of detachment and generosity?
> Do I sacrifice for others?

*Blessed are they who mourn, for they will be comforted.*

> Do I console and help those who mourn and suffer?
> Do I show compassion?

*Blessed are the meek, for they will inherit the land.*

> Am I authentically humble and self-giving?
> Have I been egotistical or boastful?

*Blessed are they who hunger and thirst for holiness, for they will be satisfied.*

> Am I passionate for the things of God?
> Do I work for the triumph of love, peace, and justice?

*Blessed are the merciful, for they will be shown mercy.*

> Am I forgiving and merciful?
> Do I give others the benefit of the doubt?
> Am I harsh or judgmental?

*Blessed are the pure of heart, for they will see God.*

> Am I single-minded in the practice of my faith?
> Have I allowed a particular sin or vice to distract me from God?

*Blessed are the peacemakers, for they will be called children of God.*

> Am I a person of reconciliation, peace, and mercy?
> Do I hold grudges or seek revenge?

*Blessed are they who are persecuted, for theirs is the kingdom of heaven.*

> Do I suffer well?
> Am I willing to sacrifice anything for my faith?
> Do I allow human respect to keep me from being a Christian witness?

## Act of Contrition I

O my God, I am most heartily sorry for all
    my sins;
and I detest them above all things because
    they displease thee,
who art infinitely good and amiable,
and subject me to the rigors of thy justice;
and I firmly resolve, with the help of thy
    grace, to do penance for them,
and never more to offend thee.


## Act of Contrition II

O my God, with all my heart I am sorry for
    having sinned against You,
not because I fear the punishment my sins
    deserve,
but because You are so good
and because I owe to You everything good
    that I have ever had.

St. Julie Billiart

# Prayer of Heartfelt Penitence and Thanksgiving

Behold, the eye of the LORD is on those who fear him,
    on those who hope in his merciful love,
that he may deliver their soul from death,
    and keep them alive in famine.

Our soul waits for the LORD;
    he is our help and shield.
Yes, our heart is glad in him,
    because we trust in his holy name.
Let your mercy, O LORD, be upon us,
    even as we hope in you.

Psalm 33:18–22

# O LORD, You Have Searched

O LORD, you have searched me and known me!

Psalm 139:1

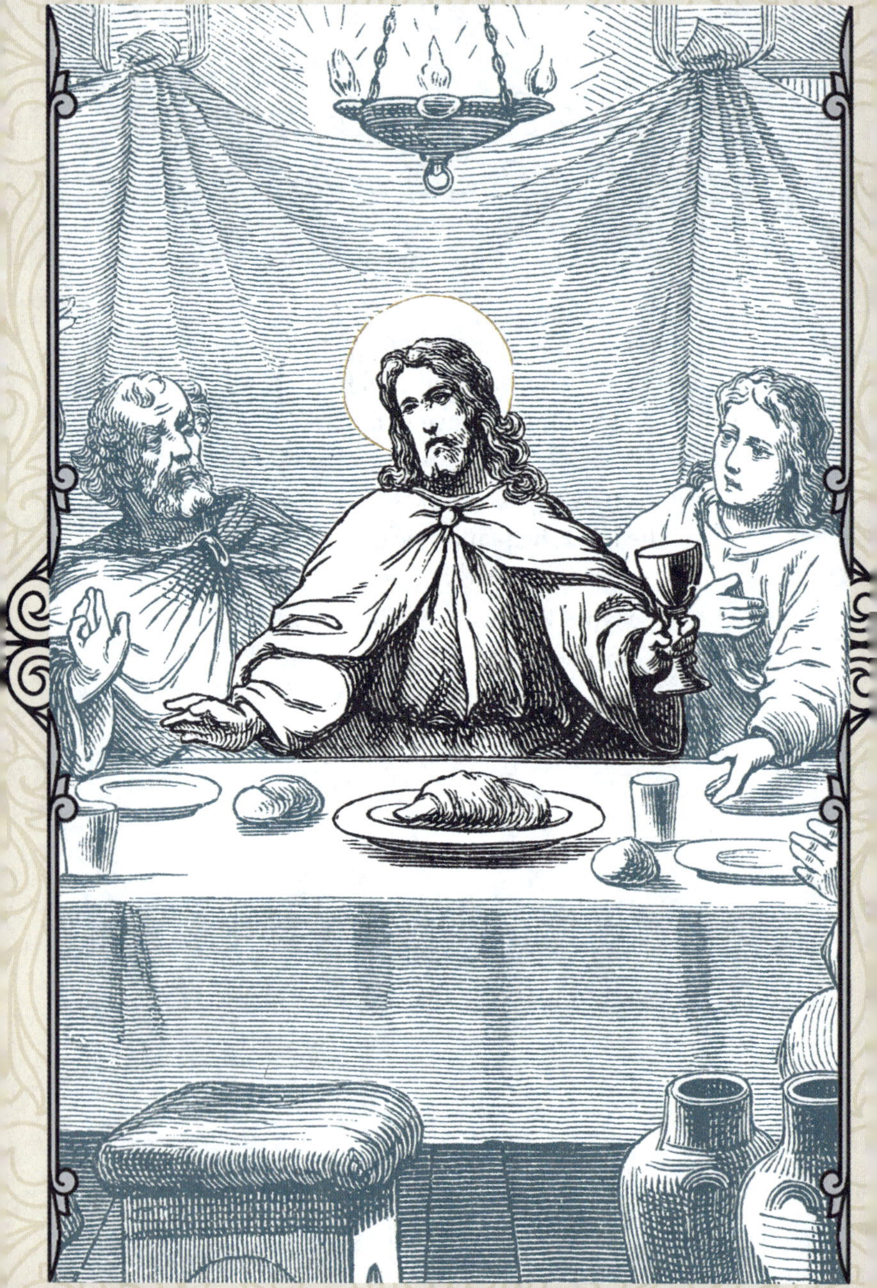

# Prayers for the Holy Eucharist

*For my flesh is food indeed, and my blood is drink indeed. He who eats my flesh and drinks my blood abides in me, and I in him.*
—John 6:55–56

| | | |
|---|---|---|
| 49. | Prayer before Mass—St. Thomas Aquinas | 62 |
| 50. | Thanks Be to God—2 Corinthians 9:15 | 63 |
| 51. | This Morning My Soul Is Greater Than the World—St. Margaret of Cortona | 64 |
| 52. | Bread of Heaven—St. Frances Xavier Cabrini | 64 |
| 53. | Anima Christi—St. Ignatius of Loyola | 65 |
| 54. | Prayer of Thanksgiving—Attributed to St. Thomas Aquinas | 66 |

# Prayer before Mass

Almighty and ever-living God,
I approach the sacrament
of your only-begotten Son
Our Lord Jesus Christ,
I come sick to the doctor of life,
unclean to the fountain of mercy,
blind to the radiance of eternal light,
and poor and needy to the Lord
of heaven and earth.

Lord, in your great generosity,
heal my sickness,
wash away my defilement,
enlighten my blindness, enrich my poverty,
and clothe my nakedness.
May I receive the bread of angels,
the King of kings and Lord of lords,
with humble reverence,
with the purity and faith,
the repentance and love,
and the determined purpose
that will help to bring me to salvation.
May I receive the sacrament
of the Lord's Body and Blood,
and its reality and power.

Kind God,
may I receive the Body
of your only-begotten Son,
our Lord Jesus Christ,
born from the womb of the Virgin Mary,
and so be received into his mystical body
and numbered among his members.

Loving Father,
as on my earthly pilgrimage
I now receive your beloved Son
under the veil of a sacrament,
may I one day see him face to face in glory,
who lives and reigns with you forever.
Amen.

*St. Thomas Aquinas*

# Thanks Be to God

Thanks be to God for his inexpressible gift!
*2 Corinthians 9:15*

## This Morning My Soul Is Greater Than the World

This morning my soul is greater than the world since it possesses You, You whom heaven and earth do not contain.

St. Margaret of Cortona

## Bread of Heaven

Bread of Heaven, Bread of Love, Bread of Life shall never be lacking from God's little orphaned children.

St. Frances Xavier Cabrini

# *Anima Christi*

Soul of Christ, sanctify me.
Body of Christ, save me.
Blood of Christ, inebriate me.
Water from the side of Christ, wash me.
Passion of Christ, strengthen me.
O good Jesus, hear me.
Within thy wounds hide me.
Separated from thee let me never be.
From the malignant enemy, defend me.
At the hour of death, call me.
And close to thee bid me.
That with thy saints I may be praising thee,
    forever and ever. Amen.

St. Ignatius of Loyola

# Prayer of Thanksgiving

Lord, Father all-powerful and ever-living God,
I thank you, for even though I am a sinner,
your unprofitable servant, not because of my worth
but in the kindness of your mercy,
you have fed me with the Precious Body and Blood
of your Son, our Lord Jesus Christ.
I pray that this Holy Communion may not bring me
condemnation and punishment but forgiveness and salvation.
May it be a helmet of faith and a shield of good will.
May it purify me from evil ways and put an end to my evil passions.
May it bring me charity and patience, humility and obedience,
and growth in the power to do good.
May it be my strong defense against all my enemies, visible and invisible,
and the perfect calming of all my evil impulses, bodily and spiritual.

May it unite me more closely to you, the
    One true God, and lead me
safely through death to everlasting happiness
    with you.
And I pray that you will lead me, a sinner, to
    the banquet where you,
with your Son and Holy Spirit, are true and
    perfect light,
total fulfillment, everlasting joy, gladness
    without end,
and perfect happiness to your saints.
Grant this through Christ our Lord,
Amen.

                Attributed to St. Thomas Aquinas

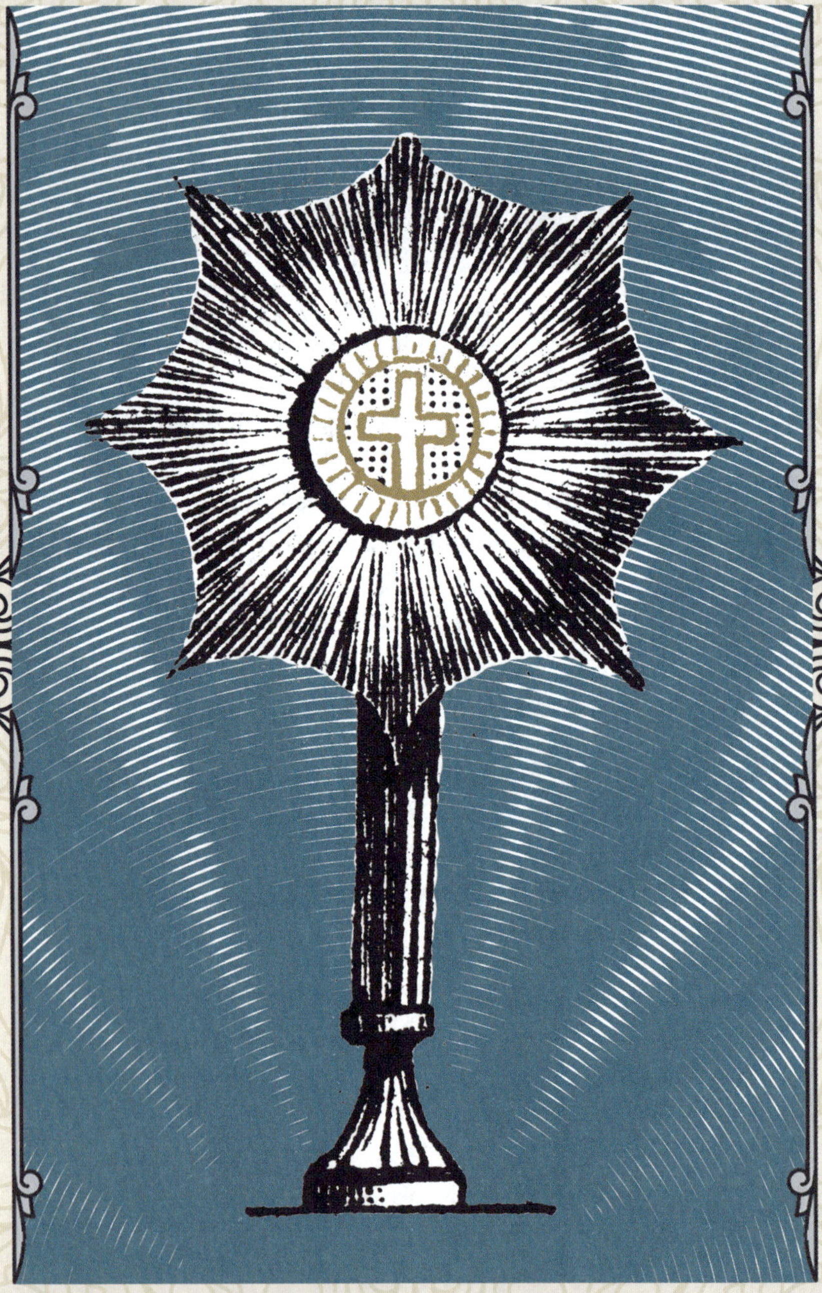

# Prayers for Adoration of the Blessed Sacrament

God is with me, I want nothing on earth.
—Ven. Pierre Toussaint

| | | |
|---|---|---|
| 55. | A Day in Your Courts Is Better Than a Thousand Elsewhere—Psalm 84:10 | 71 |
| 56. | Here Am I—Exodus 3:4 | 71 |
| 57. | Speak, Lord, for Your Servant Hears—1 Samuel 3:9 | 72 |
| 58. | Your Face Is the Only Fatherland for Me—St. Thérèse of Lisieux | 72 |

| | | |
|---|---|---|
| 59. | O Salutaris Hostia (O Saving Victim)—<br>St. Thomas Aquinas | 73 |
| 60. | Tantum Ergo—St. Thomas Aquinas | 74 |
| 61. | The Divine Praises | 76 |

## A Day in Your Courts Is Better Than a Thousand Elsewhere

A day in your courts is better than a thousand elsewhere.

Psalm 84:10

## Here Am I

Here am I.

Exodus 3:4

## Speak, LORD, for Your Servant Hears

Speak, LORD, for your servant hears.
1 Samuel 3:9

## Your Face Is the Only Fatherland for Me

Your face is the only fatherland for me.
St. Thérèse of Lisieux

# *O Salutaris Hostia*
## *(O Saving Victim)*

O Saving Victim, opening wide
The gate of heaven to man below
Our foes press on from every side;
Thine aide supply, thy strength bestow.

To thy great name be endless praise,
Immortal Godhead, one in three;
Oh, grant us endless length of days
In our true native land with thee.
Amen.

St. Thomas Aquinas

# Tantum Ergo

Down in adoration falling,
Lo, the sacred Host we hail;
Lo, o'er ancient forms departing,
Newer rites of grace prevail;
Faith for all defects supplying
Where the feeble senses fail.

To the everlasting Father,
And the Son who reigns on high,
With the Holy Ghost proceeding
Forth from each eternally,
Be salvation, honor, blessing,
Might and endless majesty.

Thou didst give them bread from heaven.
 Alleluia.
R. Containing in itself all sweetness. Alleluia.

Let us pray.
O God, who under a wonderful Sacrament hast left us a memorial of thy passion; grant us, we beseech thee, so to venerate the sacred mysteries of thy Body and Blood, that we may ever feel within us the fruit of thy

redemption. Who livest and reignest for ever and ever. Amen.

St. Thomas Aquinas

# The Divine Praises

Blessed be God.

Blessed be his holy Name.

Blessed be Jesus Christ, true God and true Man.

Blessed be the name of Jesus.

Blessed be his most Sacred Heart.

Blessed be his most Precious Blood.

Blessed be Jesus in the most holy Sacrament of the altar.

Blessed be the Holy Spirit, the Paraclete.

Blessed be the great Mother of God, Mary most holy.

Blessed be her holy and Immaculate Conception.

Blessed be her glorious Assumption.

Blessed be the name of Mary, Virgin and Mother.

Blessed be Saint Joseph, her most chaste spouse.

Blessed be God in his angels and in his saints.

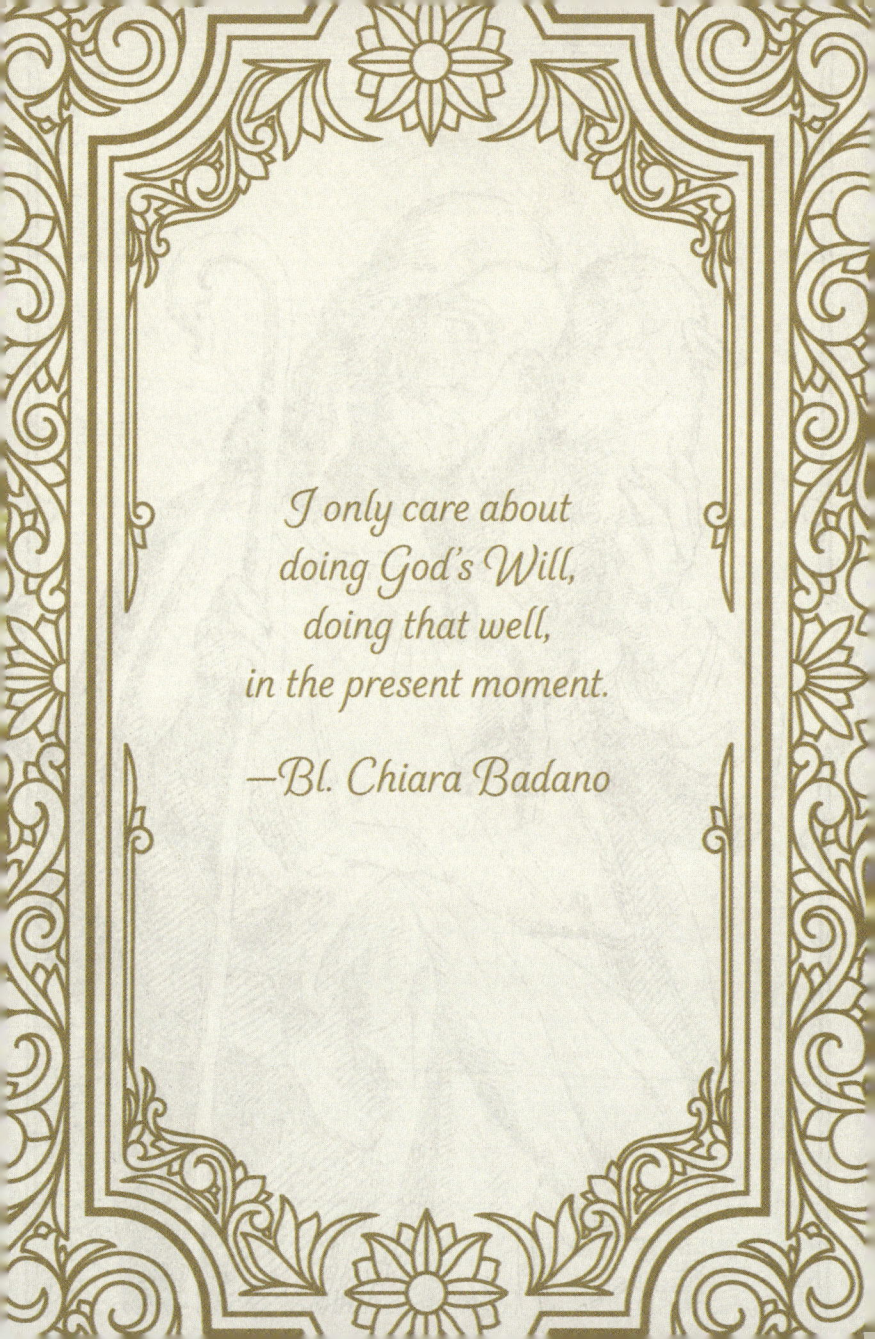

*I only care about
doing God's Will,
doing that well,
in the present moment.*

—Bl. Chiara Badano

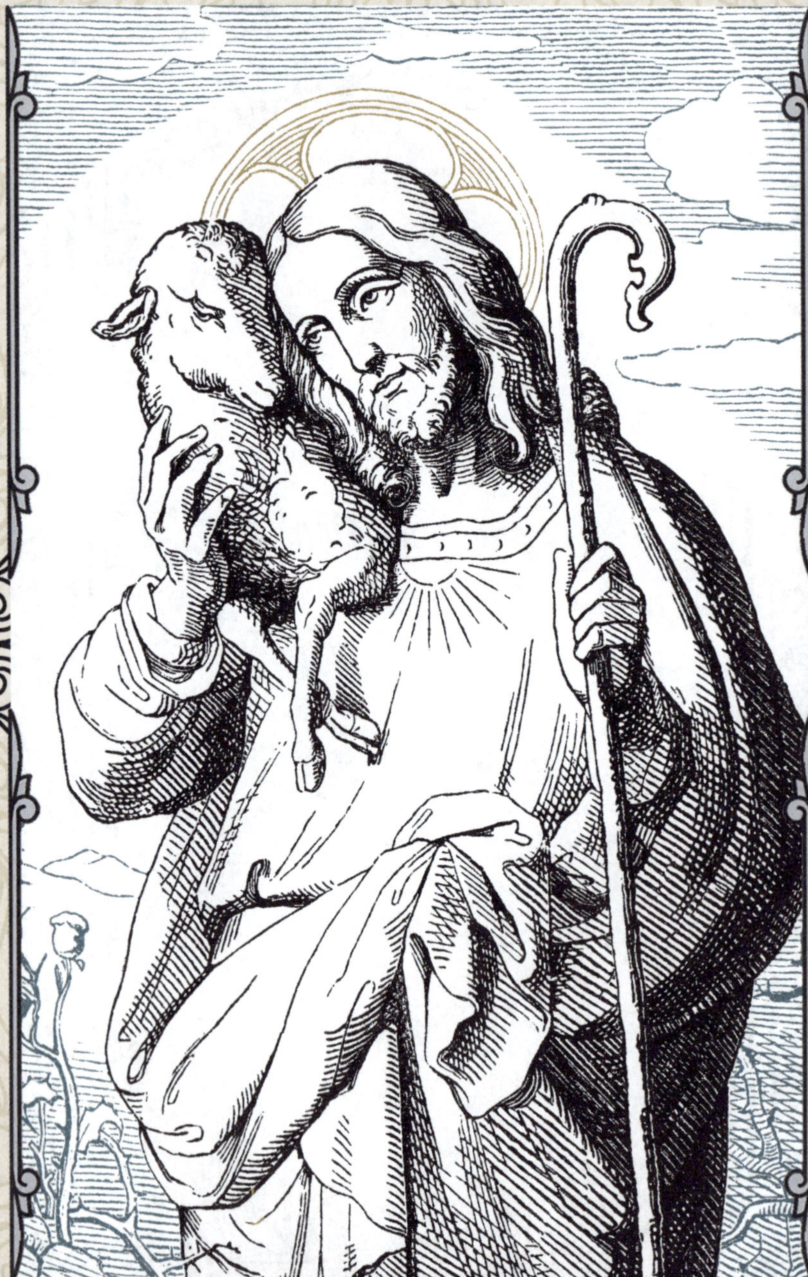

# Prayers and Devotions to Jesus Christ

> I look at him and he looks at me.
> —St. John Vianney

| | | |
|---|---|---|
| 62. | St. Patrick's Breastplate | 81 |
| 63. | Take My Heart, Dear Lord— St. Lutgarde of Aywieres | 82 |
| 64. | Act of Consecration to the Sacred Heart of Jesus—St. Margaret Mary Alacoque | 83 |
| 65. | O Heart of Love— St. Margaret Mary Alacoque | 84 |
| 66. | Litany of the Sacred Heart of Jesus | 85 |
| 67. | Divine Mercy Chaplet | 89 |

| | | |
|---|---|---|
| 68. | Prayer before a Crucifix | 90 |
| 69. | Prayer before the Crucifix at San Damiano—St. Francis of Assisi | 91 |
| 70. | Behold the Cross of the Lord—St. Anthony of Padua | 91 |
| 71. | Prayer to Christ the King | 92 |

# St. Patrick's Breastplate

I arise today
Through a mighty strength, the invocation
    of the Trinity,
Through belief in the Threeness,
Through confession of the Oneness
of the Creator of creation.
I arise today
Through the strength of Christ's birth with
    His baptism,
Through the strength of His crucifixion with
    His burial,
Through the strength of His resurrection
    with His ascension,
Through the strength of His descent for the
    judgment of doom.
I arise today. . . .
Christ with me,
Christ before me,
Christ behind me,
Christ in me,
Christ beneath me,
Christ above me,
Christ on my right,
Christ on my left,
Christ when I lie down,

Christ when I sit down,
Christ when I arise,
Christ in the heart of every man who thinks
    of me,
Christ in the mouth of everyone who speaks
    of me,
Christ in every eye that sees me,
Christ in every ear that hears me.
I arise today
Through a mighty strength, the invocation
    of the Trinity,
Through belief in the Threeness,
Through confession of the Oneness
of the Creator of creation.

St. Patrick

## Take My Heart, Dear Lord

Take my heart, dear Lord. May your heart's love be so mingled and united with my heart that I may possess my heart in you. May it ever remain there safe in your protection.

St. Lutgarde of Aywieres

# Act of Consecration to the Sacred Heart of Jesus

O Sacred Heart of Jesus, to thee I consecrate and offer up my person and my life, my actions, trials, and sufferings, that my entire being may henceforth only be employed in loving, honoring, and glorifying thee. This is my irrevocable will, to belong entirely to thee, and to do all for thy love, renouncing with my whole heart all that can displease thee.

I take thee, O Sacred Heart, for the sole object of my love, the protection of my life, the pledge of my salvation, the remedy of my frailty and inconstancy, the reparation for all the defects of my life, and my secure refuge at the hour of my death. Be thou, O Most Merciful Heart, my justification before God thy Father, and screen me from his anger which I have so justly merited. I fear all from my own weakness and malice, but placing my entire confidence in thee, O Heart of Love, I hope all from thine infinite Goodness. Annihilate in me all that can displease or resist thee. Imprint thy pure love so deeply in my heart that I may never forget thee or be separated from thee.

I beseech thee, through infinite Goodness, grant that my name be engraved upon thy Heart, for in this I place all my happiness and all my glory, to live and to die as one of thy devoted servants. Amen.

St. Margaret Mary Alacoque

## O Heart of Love

O Heart of Love,
I put all my trust in you.
For I fear all things from my own weakness
but I hope for all things from your goodness.
Had I a thousand bodies, O my God,
a thousand loves and a thousand lives,
I would immolate them all to your service.

St. Margaret Mary Alacoque

# Litany of the Sacred Heart of Jesus

Lord, have mercy.
*Lord have mercy.*
Christ, have mercy.
*Christ, have mercy.*
Lord, have mercy.
*Lord, have mercy.*

God our Father in heaven, *have mercy on us.*
God the Son, Redeemer of the world, *have mercy on us.*
God the Holy Spirit, *have mercy on us.*
Holy Trinity, one God, *have mercy on us.*
Heart of Jesus, Son of the eternal Father, *have mercy on us.*
Heart of Jesus, formed by the Holy Spirit in the womb of the Virgin Mother, *have mercy on us.*
Heart of Jesus, one with the eternal Word, *have mercy on us.*
Heart of Jesus, infinite in majesty, *have mercy on us.*
Heart of Jesus, holy temple of God, *have mercy on us.*

Heart of Jesus, tabernacle of the Most High, *have mercy on us.*

Heart of Jesus, house of God and gate of heaven, *have mercy on us.*

Heart of Jesus, aflame with love for us, *have mercy on us.*

Heart of Jesus, source of justice and love, *have mercy on us.*

Heart of Jesus, full of goodness and love, *have mercy on us.*

Heart of Jesus, wellspring of all virtue, *have mercy on us.*

Heart of Jesus, worthy of all praise, *have mercy on us.*

Heart of Jesus, king and center of all hearts, *have mercy on us.*

Heart of Jesus, treasure-house of wisdom and knowledge, *have mercy on us.*

Heart of Jesus, in whom there dwells the fullness of God, *have mercy on us.*

Heart of Jesus, in whom the Father is well pleased, *have mercy on us.*

Heart of Jesus, from whose fullness we have all received, *have mercy on us.*

Heart of Jesus, desire of the eternal hills, *have mercy on us.*

Heart of Jesus, patient and full of mercy, *have mercy on us*.

Heart of Jesus, generous to all who turn to you, *have mercy on us*.

Heart of Jesus, fountain of life and holiness, *have mercy on us*.

Heart of Jesus, atonement for our sins, *have mercy on us*.

Heart of Jesus, overwhelmed with insults, *have mercy on us*.

Heart of Jesus, broken for our sins, *have mercy on us*.

Heart of Jesus, obedient even to death, *have mercy on us*.

Heart of Jesus, pierced by a lance, *have mercy on us*.

Heart of Jesus, source of all consolation, *have mercy on us*.

Heart of Jesus, our life and resurrection, *have mercy on us*.

Heart of Jesus, our peace and reconciliation, *have mercy on us*.

Heart of Jesus, victim of our sins, *have mercy on us*.

Heart of Jesus, salvation of all who trust in you, *have mercy on us*.

Heart of Jesus, delight of all the saints, *have mercy on us.*

Lamb of God, you take away the sins of the world, *have mercy on us.*
Lamb of God, you take away the sins of the world, *have mercy on us.*
Lamb of God, you take away the sins of the world, *have mercy on us.*

Jesus, gentle and humble of heart.
*Touch our hearts and make them like your own.*

Let us pray.
Grant, we pray, almighty God,
that we, who glory in the Heart of your beloved Son
and recall the wonders of his love for us,
may be made worthy to receive
an overflowing measure of grace
from that fount of heavenly gifts.
Through Christ our Lord.
Amen.

# Divine Mercy Chaplet

Eternal Father, I offer you the Body and Blood, Soul and Divinity of your dearly beloved Son, Our Lord, Jesus Christ, in atonement for our sins and those of the whole world. (*Pray on the "Our Father" beads of the rosary*).

For the sake of his sorrowful Passion, have mercy on us and on the whole world. (*Pray on the "Hail Mary" beads of the rosary*).

Holy God, Holy Might One, Holy Immortal One, have mercy on us and on the whole world. (*Pray three times at the end of five decades*).

# Prayer before a Crucifix

Look down upon me, good and gentle Jesus,
while before thy face I humbly kneel, and
with burning soul
pray and beseech thee
to fix deep in my heart lively sentiments
of faith, hope, and charity,
true contrition for my sins,
and a firm purpose of amendment;
while I contemplate
with great love and tender pity
thy five wounds, pondering over them within
    me,
and calling to mind the words which David,
thy prophet, said of thee, my good Jesus:
"They have pierced my hands and my feet;
They have numbered all my bones."

# Prayer before the Crucifix at San Damiano

Most High, glorious God, enlighten the darkness of my heart
and give me true faith, certain hope, and perfect charity, sense and knowledge,
Lord, that I may carry out your holy and true command.
Amen.

St. Francis of Assisi

# Behold the Cross of the Lord

Behold the Cross of the Lord!
Begone, you enemy powers!
The Lion of the Tribe of Judah,
The Root of David, has conquered.
Alleluia!

St. Anthony of Padua

# Prayer to Christ the King

O Christ Jesus, I acknowledge thee
to be the King of the universe:
all that has been made is created for thee.
Exercise over me all thy sovereign rights.

I hereby renew the promises of my Baptism,
renouncing Satan and all his works and
> pomps,
and I engage myself to lead henceforth a
> truly Christian life.
And in an especial manner do I undertake
> to bring about
the triumph of the rights of God
and thy Church, so far as in me lies.

Divine Heart of Jesus, I offer thee
my poor actions to obtain the
> acknowledgment
by every heart of thy sacred Kingly power.
In such wise may the kingdom of thy peace
be firmly established throughout all the
> earth.
Amen.

*Jesus looking upon him loved him.*

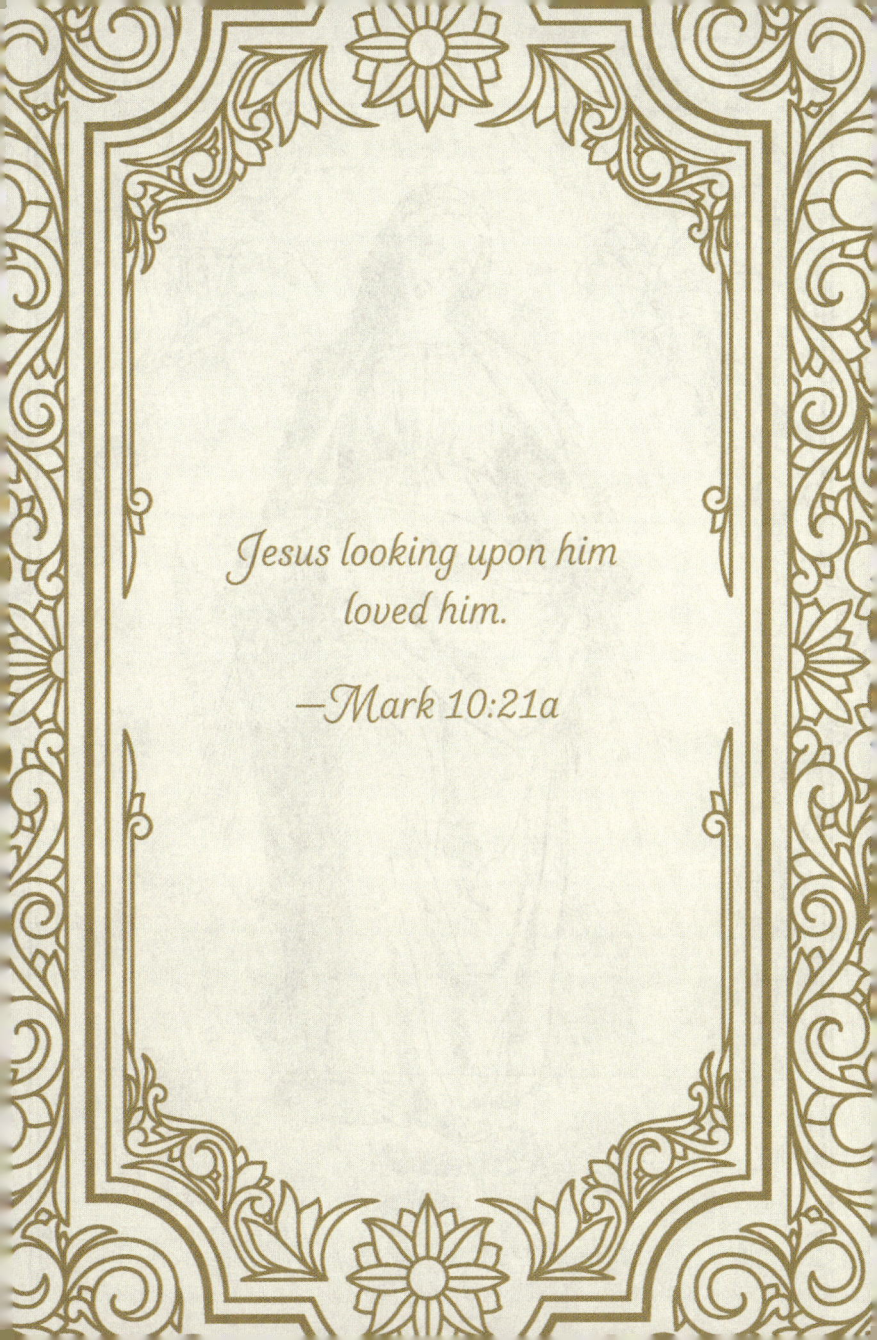

—Mark 10:21a

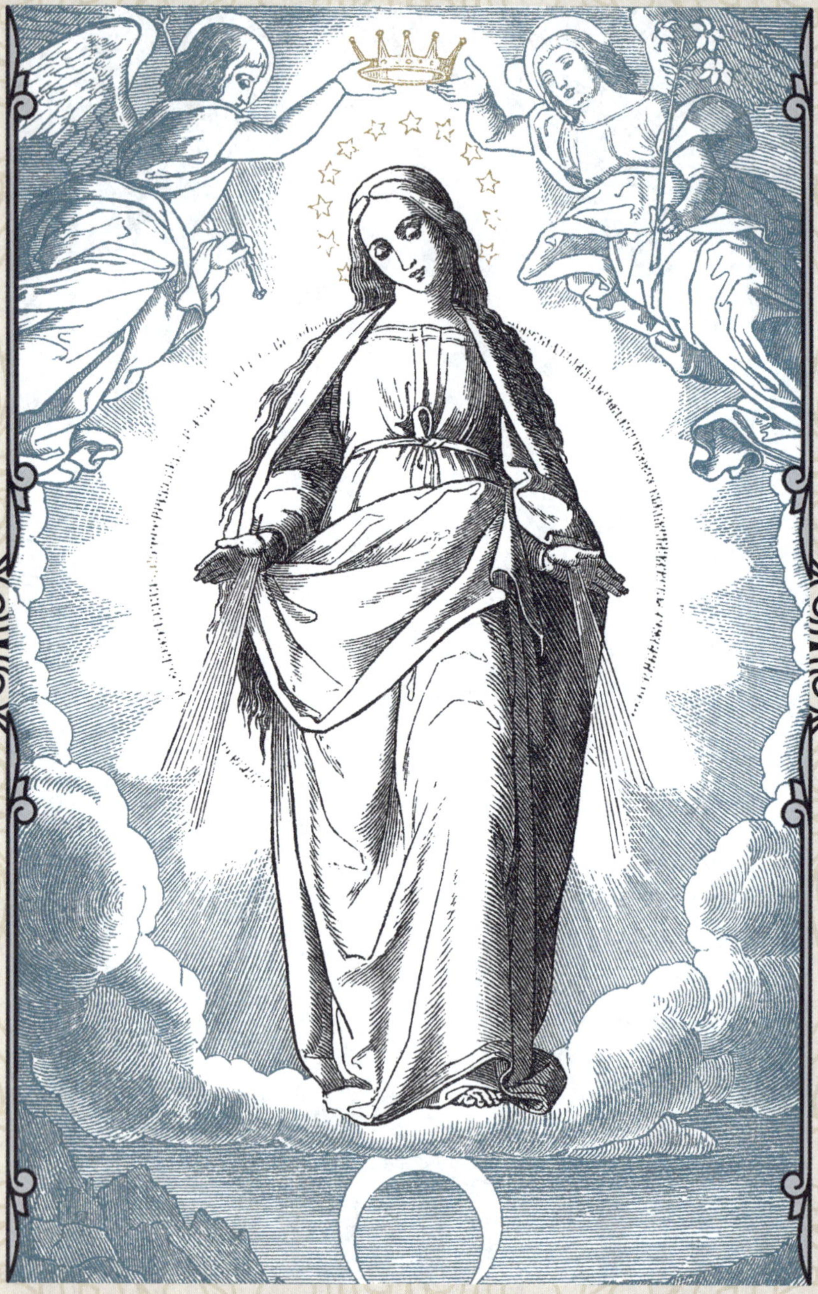

# Prayers and Devotions to the Blessed Virgin Mary

> Mother, I am yours now and forever. Through you and with you I always want to belong completely to Jesus.
>
> —Fr. Dolindo Ruotolo

| | | |
|---|---|---|
| 72. | Mary, I Love You—St. Philip Neri | 97 |
| 73. | Stabat Mater | 98 |
| 74. | Ave Maris Stella | 101 |
| 75. | The Litany of Loreto | 103 |
| 76. | Memorare—St. Bernard of Clairvaux | 106 |
| 77. | Act of Entrustment to Mary—St. John Paul II | 107 |

| | | |
|---|---|---|
| 78. | Totus Tuus Prayer—St. John Paul II | 110 |
| 79. | Prayer to Our Lady of Guadalupe, Patroness of the Americas | 111 |
| 80. | The Holy Rosary | 113 |

  a. *The Joyful Mysteries*

  b. *The Sorrowful Mysteries*

  c. *The Glorious Mysteries*

  d. *The Luminous Mysteries (Mysteries of Light)*

# Mary, I Love You

Mary, I love you.

Mary, make me live in God, with God, and for God.

Draw me after you, holy mother.

O Mary, may your children persevere in loving you.

Mary, Mother of God and mother of mercy, pray for me and for the departed.

Mary, holy Mother of God, be our helper.

In every difficulty and distress, come to our aid, O Mary.

O Queen of Heaven, lead us to eternal life with God.

Mother of God, remember me, and help me always to remember you.

O Mary, conceived without sin,

pray for us who have recourse to you.

Pray for us, O holy Mother of God,

that we may be made worthy of the promises of Christ.

Holy Mary, Mother of God, pray to Jesus for me.

St. Philip Neri

# Stabat Mater

At the Cross her station keeping,
Stood the mournful Mother weeping,
Close to Jesus to the last:

Through her heart, his sorrow sharing,
All his bitter anguish bearing,
now at length the sword has passed.

Oh, how sad and sore distressed
Was that Mother highly blest
Of the sole-begotten One!

Christ above in torment hangs;
She beneath beholds the pangs
Of her dying glorious Son.

Is there one who would not weep,
Whelmed in miseries so deep,
Christ's dear Mother to behold?

Can the human heart refrain
From partaking in her pain,
In that Mother's pain untold?

Bruised, derided, cursed, defiled,
She beheld her tender Child
All with bloody scourges rent;

For the sins of his own nation,
Saw him hang in desolation
Till his Spirit forth he sent.

O thou Mother! Fount of love!
Touch my spirit from above,
Make my heart with thine accord:

Make me feel as thou hast felt;
Make my soul to glow and melt
With the love of Christ my Lord.

Holy Mother! Pierce me through;
In my heart each wound renew
Of my Savior crucified:

Let me share with thee his pain,
Who for all my sins was slain,
Who for me in torments died.

Let me mingle tears with thee,
Mourning him who mourned for me,
All the days that I may live:

By the Cross with thee to stay;
There with thee to weep and pray,
Is all I ask of thee to give.

Virgin of all virgins blest!
Listen to my fond request:
Let me share thy grief divine;

Let me, to my latest breath,
In my body bear the death
Of that dying Son of thine.

Wounded with his every wound,
Steep my soul till it hath swooned,
In his very blood away;

Be to me, O Virgin, nigh,
Lest in flames I burn and die,
In his awful Judgment day.

Christ, when thou shalt call me hence,
Be thy Mother my defense,
Be thy Cross my victory;

While my body here decays,
May my soul thy goodness praise,
Safe in Paradise with thee.

# Ave Maris Stella

Hail, you Star of the Ocean!
Portal of the sky, Ever Virgin Mother,
Of the Lord most high.
O! by Gabriel's Ave,
Uttered long ago,
Eva's name reversing,
Establish peace below.
Break the captive's fetters;
Light on blindness pour;
All our ills expelling,
Every bliss implore.
Show yourself a mother;
Offer him our sighs,
Who for us Incarnate
Did not you despise.
Virgin of all virgins!
To your shelter take us;
Gentlest of the gentle!
Chaste and gentle make us.
Still as on we journey,
Help our weak endeavor,
Till with you and Jesus
We rejoice forever.
Through the highest heaven,
To the Almighty Three,

Father, Son, and Spirit,
One same glory be.

# The Litany of Loreto

We fly to thy patronage, O holy Mother of God! Despise not our petitions in our necessities, but deliver us from all dangers, O ever-glorious and blessed Virgin!

Lord, have mercy on us.
*Christ, have mercy on us.*
Lord, have mercy on us. Christ, hear us.
*Christ, graciously hear us.*
God, the Father of heaven, *have mercy on us.*
God the Son, Redeemer of the world, *have mercy on us.*
God the Holy Spirit, *have mercy on us.*
Holy Trinity, one God, *have mercy on us.*
Holy Mary, *pray for us.*
Holy Mother of God, *pray for us.*
Holy Virgin of virgins, *pray for us.*
Mother of Christ, *pray for us.*
Mother of divine grace, *pray for us.*
Mother most pure, *pray for us.*
Mother most chaste, *pray for us.*
Mother inviolate, *pray for us.*
Mother undefiled, *pray for us.*
Mother most amiable, *pray for us.*
Mother most admirable, *pray for us.*

Mother of our Creator, *pray for us*.
Mother of our Redeemer, *pray for us*.
Virgin most prudent, *pray for us*.
Virgin most venerable, *pray for us*.
Virgin most renowned, *pray for us*.
Virgin most powerful, *pray for us*.
Virgin most merciful, *pray for us*.
Virgin most faithful, *pray for us*.
Mirror of justice, *pray for us*.
Seat of wisdom, *pray for us*.
Cause of our joy, *pray for us*.
Spiritual vessel, *pray for us*.
Vessel of honor, *pray for us*.
Vessel of singular devotion, *pray for us*.
Mystical rose, *pray for us*.
Tower of David, *pray for us*.
Tower of ivory, *pray for us*.
House of gold, *pray for us*.
Ark of the covenant, *pray for us*.
Gate of heaven, *pray for us*.
Morning star, *pray for us*.
Health of the weak, *pray for us*.
Refuge of sinners, *pray for us*.
Comfort of the afflicted, *pray for us*.
Help of Christians, *pray for us*.
Queen of Angels, *pray for us*.
Queen of Patriarchs, *pray for us*.

Queen of Prophets, *pray for us.*
Queen of Apostles, *pray for us.*
Queen of Martyrs, *pray for us.*
Queen of Confessors, *pray for us.*
Queen of Virgins, *pray for us.*
Queen of all Saints, *pray for us.*
Queen conceived without sin, *pray for us.*
Queen of the most holy Rosary, *pray for us.*
Lamb of God, who takes away the sins of the world, *spare us, O Lord.*
Lamb of God, who takes away the sins of the world, *graciously hear us, O Lord.*
Lamb of God, who takes away the sins of the world, *have mercy on us.*
Pray for us, O holy Mother of God.
*That we may be made worthy of the promises of Christ.*

Let us pray.

Defend, O Lord, we beseech thee, by the intercession of the blessed Mary ever virgin, this thy family from all adversity; and mercifully protect us, who prostrate ourselves before thee with all our hearts, from the snares of the enemy. Through Christ our Lord.

Pour forth, we beseech thee, O Lord, thy grace into our hearts, that we to whom the Incarnation of Christ, thy Son, has been made known by the message of an angel, may, by his Passion and Cross, be brought to the glory of his resurrection. Through the same Christ our Lord. Amen.

## *Memorare*

Remember, O most gracious Virgin Mary,
that never was it known
that anyone who fled to thy protection,
implored thy help, or sought thy intercession
was left unaided.
Inspired by this confidence,
I fly unto thee, O Virgin of virgins, my
    Mother;
to thee do I come, before thee I stand, sinful
    and sorrowful.
O Mother of the World Incarnate,
despise not my petitions,
but in thy mercy, hear and answer me.
St. Bernard of Clairvaux

# Act of Entrustment to Mary

"Behold, your Mother!" (John 19:27)
O Virgin Mary,
Jesus on the Cross
wanted to entrust us to you,
not to lessen
but to reaffirm
his exclusive role as Savior
of the world.

If in the disciple John
all the children of the Church were
    entrusted to you,
the happier I am to see
the young people of the world
entrusted to you, O Mary.
To you, gentle Mother,
whose protection I have always experienced,
this evening I entrust them to you once
    again.
All seek refuge and
protection under your mantle.
You, Mother of divine grace,
make them shine with
the beauty of Christ!

The young people of this century,
at the dawn of the new millennium, still live
    the torment that derives from sin,
from hatred, from violence,
from terrorism and from war.
But it is also the young to whom the Church
    looks confidently, knowing
that with the help of God's grace,
they will succeed in believing and in living as
    Gospel witnesses
in present-day history.

O Mary, help them to respond to their
    vocation.
Guide them to the knowledge of true love
and bless their affections.
Support them in times of suffering.
Make them fearless heralds
of Christ's greeting on Easter Day: Peace
    be with you!
With them, I also entrust myself
once again to you
and with confident affection
I repeat to you:
*Totus Tuus ego sum!*
I am all yours!

And each one of them
cries to you, with me:
*Totus Tuus!*
*Totus Tuus!*
Amen.

> St. John Paul II

# Totus Tuus Prayer

Immaculate Conception, Mary, my Mother,
Live in me. Act in me.
Speak in and through me.
Think your thoughts in my mind. Love,
 through my heart.
Give me your dispositions and feelings.
Teach, lead and guide me to Jesus.
Correct, enlighten and expand my thoughts
 and behavior.
Possess my soul. Take over my entire personality and life.
Replace it with yourself.
Incline me to constant adoration and
 thanksgiving.
Pray in me and through me.
Let me live in you and keep me in this union
 always.

St. John Paul II

# Prayer to Our Lady of Guadalupe, Patroness of the Americas

O God our Creator,
from your provident hand we have received
our right to life, liberty, and the pursuit of
 happiness.
You have called us as your people and given
 us
the right and the duty to worship you, the
 only true God,
and your Son, Jesus Christ.
Through the power and working of your
 Holy Spirit,
you call us to live out our faith in the midst
 of the world,
bringing the light and the saving truth of
 the Gospel
to every corner of society.
We ask you to bless us
in our vigilance for the gift of religious
 liberty.
Give us the strength of mind and heart
to readily defend our freedoms when they
 are threatened;
give us courage in making our voices heard

on behalf of the rights of your Church
and the freedom of conscience of all people
   of faith.
Grant, we pray, O heavenly Father,
a clear and united voice to all your sons and
   daughters
gathered in your Church
in this decisive hour in the history of our
   nation,
so that, with every trial withstood
and every danger overcome—
for the sake of our children, our
   grandchildren,
and all who come after us—
this great land will always be "one nation,
   under God,
indivisible, with liberty and justice for all."
We ask this through Christ our Lord.
Amen.

# The Holy Rosary

*The Rosary begins with the Apostles' Creed, an Our Father, three repetitions of Hail Mary, and a Glory Be, then continues with an Our Father, ten repetitions of Hail Mary, and a Glory Be for each "decade," or group of ten beads. With each decade there is a mystery to meditate on while praying. In addition to the Joyful Mysteries, the Sorrowful Mysteries, and the Glorious Mysteries, in 2002 St. John Paul II added the Luminous Mysteries through his apostolic letter* Rosarium Virginis Mariae.

## The Joyful Mysteries

The Annunciation
The Visitation
The Nativity
The Presentation
The Finding of Jesus in the Temple

## The Sorrowful Mysteries

The Agony in the Garden
The Scourging at the Pillar
The Crowning with Thorns
The Carrying of the Cross
The Crucifixion

## The Glorious Mysteries

The Resurrection
The Ascension of Our Lord
The Descent of the Holy Spirit
The Assumption of Our Lady
The Coronation of the Blessed Virgin Mary

## The Luminous Mysteries (Mysteries of Light)

The Baptism in the Jordan
The Wedding at Cana
The Proclamation of the Kingdom
The Transfiguration
The Institution of the Eucharist

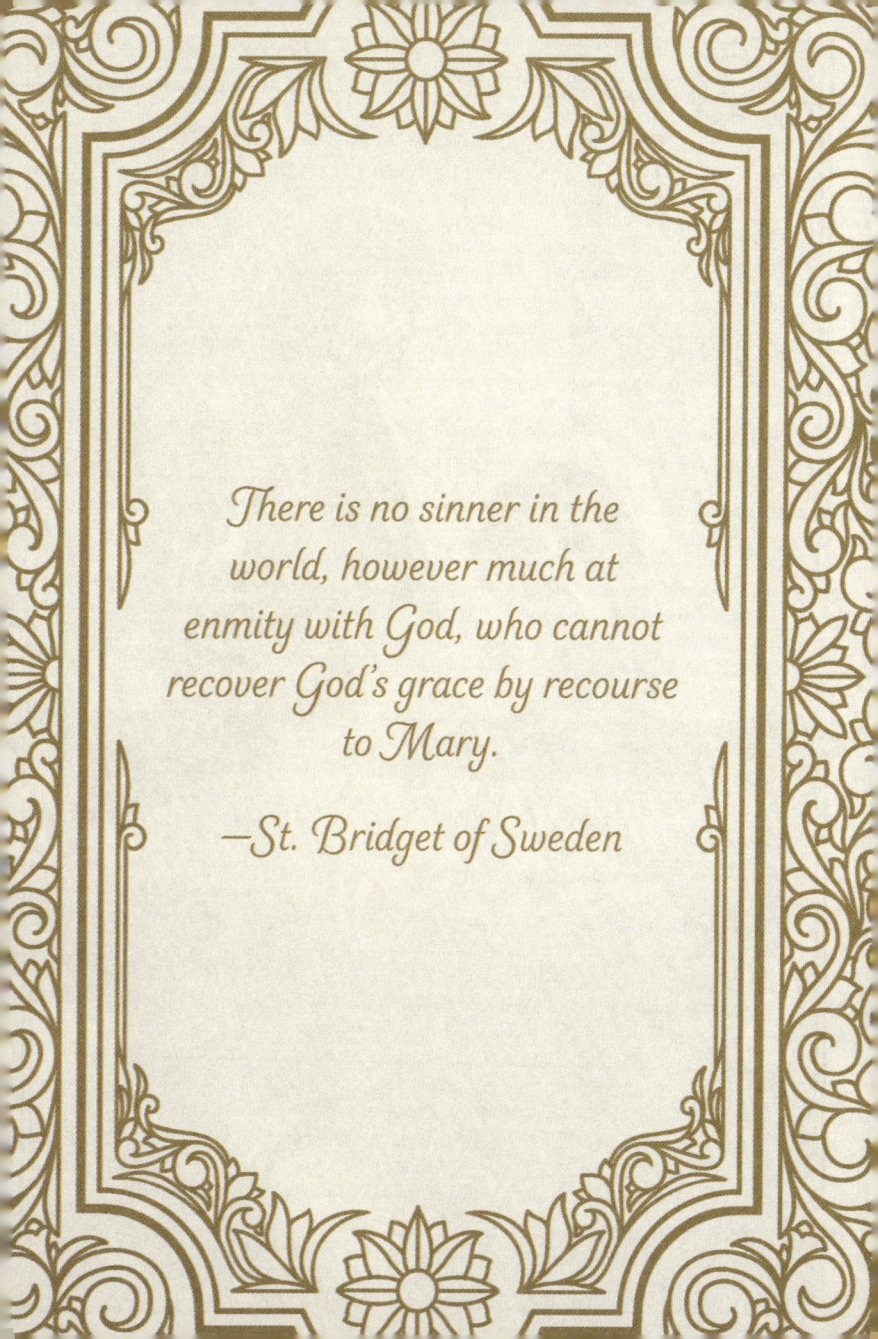

*There is no sinner in the world, however much at enmity with God, who cannot recover God's grace by recourse to Mary.*

—St. Bridget of Sweden

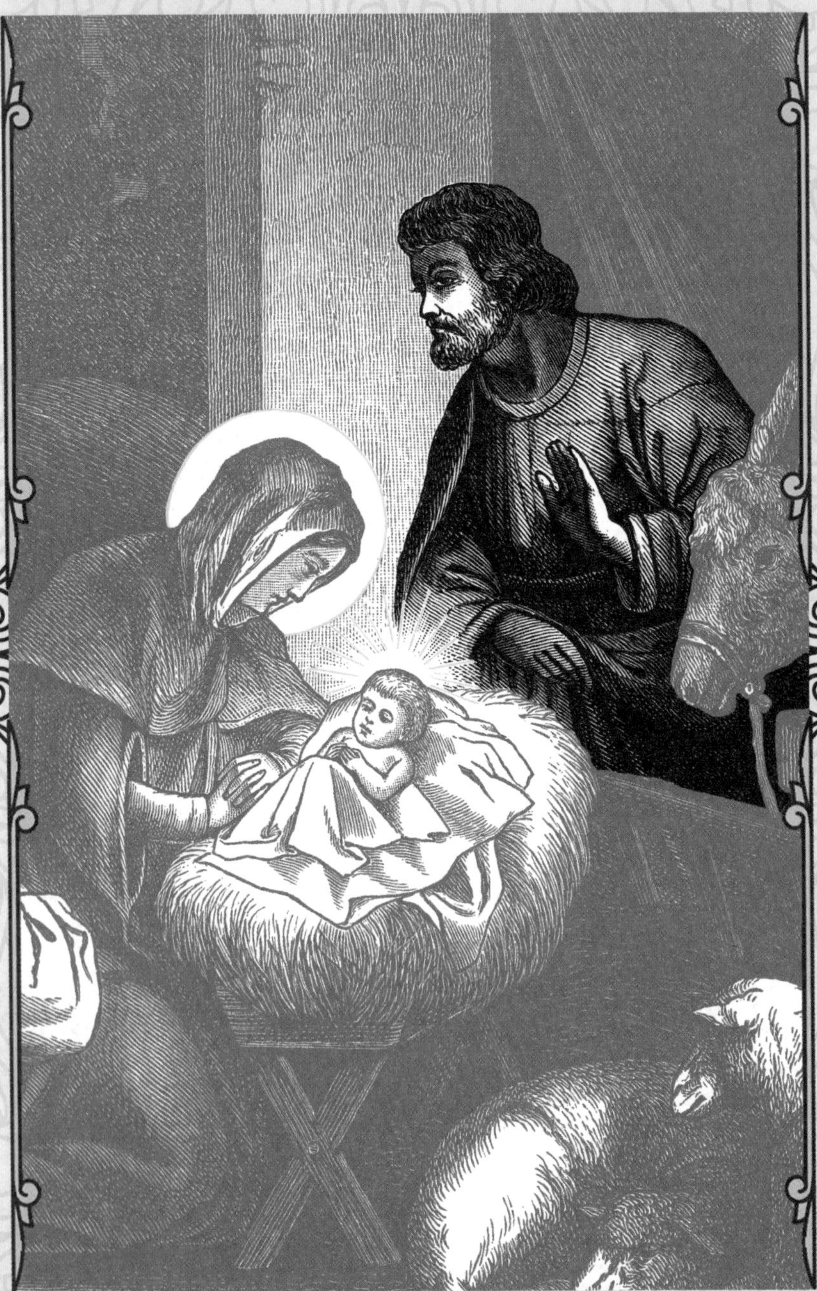

# Prayers and Devotions to St. Joseph

When you invoke St. Joseph, you don't have to say much. You know your Father in heaven knows what you need; well, so does his friend St. Joseph. Tell him, "If you were in my place, St. Joseph, what would you do? Well, pray for this on my behalf."

—St. André Bessette

| | | |
|---|---|---|
| 81. | Litany of St. Joseph | 119 |
| 82. | St. Joseph Memorare | 122 |
| 83. | Prayer to St. Joseph, Man of Silence— Pope Francis | 123 |
| 84. | Prayer to Sleeping St. Joseph | 124 |

| | | |
|---|---|---|
| 85. | St. Joseph, Just Man and Husband of Mary—Pope Francis | 125 |
| 86. | St. Joseph, Father in Tenderness—Pope Francis | 126 |
| 87. | Prayer to St. Joseph for the Protection of Workers—Pope Francis | 127 |
| 88. | St. Joseph, Guardian of the Pure in Heart | 128 |

# Litany of St. Joseph

Lord, have mercy.
*Lord, have mercy.*
Christ, have mercy.
*Christ, have mercy.*
Lord, have mercy.
*Lord, have mercy.*
Christ, hear us.
*Christ, graciously hear us.*

God the Father of heaven, *have mercy on us.*
God the Son, Redeemer of the world, *have mercy on us.*
God the Holy Spirit, *have mercy on us.*
Holy Trinity, one God, *have mercy on us.*

Holy Mary, *pray for us.*
St. Joseph, *pray for us.*
Illustrious son of David, *pray for us.*
Light of patriarchs, *pray for us.*
Spouse of the Mother of God, *pray for us.*
Guardian of the Redeemer, *pray for us.*
Pure Guardian of the Virgin, *pray for us.*
Provider for the Son of God, *pray for us.*
Zealous defender of Christ, *pray for us.*
Servant of Christ, *pray for us.*

Minister of salvation, *pray for us.*
Head of the Holy Family, *pray for us.*
Joseph, most just, *pray for us.*
Joseph, most chaste, *pray for us.*
Joseph, most prudent, *pray for us.*
Joseph, most brave, *pray for us.*
Joseph, most obedient, *pray for us.*
Joseph, most loyal, *pray for us.*
Mirror of patience, *pray for us.*
Lover of poverty, *pray for us.*
Model for workers, *pray for us.*
Glory of family life, *pray for us.*
Guardian of virgins, *pray for us.*
Cornerstone of families, *pray for us.*
Support in difficulties, *pray for us.*
Comfort of the sorrowing, *pray for us.*
Hope of the sick, *pray for us.*
Patron of exiles, *pray for us.*
Patron of the afflicted, *pray for us.*
Patron of the poor, *pray for us.*
Patron of the dying, *pray for us.*
Terror of demons, *pray for us.*
Protector of the Holy Church, *pray for us.*

Lamb of God, you take away the sins of the world.
*Spare us, O Lord.*

Lamb of God, you take away the sins of the world.
*Hear us, O Lord.*
Lamb of God, you take away the sins of the world.
*Have mercy on us.*

He made him master of his house, *and ruler of all his possessions.*

Let us pray,
O God, who in your inexpressible providence were pleased to choose St. Joseph as spouse of your most holy Mother, grant, we pray, that we, who revere him as our protector on earth, may be worthy of his heavenly intercession, who live and reign for ever and ever. Amen.

# St. Joseph Memorare

Remember, O most chaste spouse of the Virgin Mary, that never was it known that anyone who implored your help and sought your intercession was left unassisted. Full of confidence in your power I fly unto you and beg your protection. Despise not, O Guardian of the Redeemer, my humble supplication, but in your bounty, hear and answer me. Amen.

# Prayer to St. Joseph, Man of Silence

St. Joseph, man of silence,
you who in the Gospel did not utter a single word,
teach us to fast from vain words,
to rediscover the value of words that edify, encourage, console, and support.
Be close to those who suffer from words that hurt,
like slander and backbiting,
and help us always to match words with deeds. Amen.

Pope Francis

# Prayer to Sleeping St. Joseph

O St. Joseph, you are a man greatly favored by the Most High. The angel of the Lord appeared to you in dreams, while you slept, to warn you and guide you as you cared for the Holy Family. You were both silent and strong, a loyal and courageous protector.

Dear St. Joseph, as you rest in the Lord, confident of his absolute power and goodness, look upon me. Please take my need (mention your request) into your heart, dream of it, and present it to your Son. Help me then, good St. Joseph, to hear the voice of God, to arise, and act with love. I praise and thank God with joy. St. Joseph, I love you. Amen.

# St. Joseph, Just Man and Husband of Mary

St. Joseph,
you who loved Mary with freedom,
and chose to renounce your fantasies to give way to reality,
help each of us to allow ourselves to be surprised by God
and to accept life not as something unforeseen from which to defend ourselves,
but as a mystery that hides the secret of true joy.
Obtain joy and radicality for all engaged Christians,
while always being aware
that only mercy and forgiveness make love possible. Amen.

Pope Francis

# St. Joseph, Father in Tenderness

St. Joseph, father in tenderness,
teach us to accept that we are loved precisely in that which is weakest in us.
Grant that we may place no obstacle between our poverty and the greatness of God's love.
Stir in us the desire to approach to Reconciliation,
that we may be forgiven and also made capable of loving
tenderly our brothers and sisters in their poverty.
Be close to those who have done wrong and are paying the price for it.
Help them to find not only justice but also tenderness so that they can start again.
And teach them that the first way to begin again
is to sincerely ask for forgiveness, to feel the Father's caress.
Amen.

Pope Francis

# Prayer to St. Joseph for the Protection of Workers

O St. Joseph,
Patron of the Church!
You, who side by side with the Word made flesh,
worked each day to earn your bread,
drawing from Him the strength to live and to toil;
you who experienced the anxiety for the morrow,
the bitterness of poverty, the uncertainty of work:
you who today give the shining example,
humble in the eyes of men
but most exalted in the sight of God:
protect workers in their hard daily lives,
defending them from discouragement,
from negative revolt,
and from pleasure-loving temptations;
and keep peace in the world,
that peace which alone can ensure the development of peoples.
Amen.

Pope Francis

# St. Joseph, Guardian of the Pure in Heart

Gentle Joseph, God is captivated by the quality of your heart.
Your entire being is focused on doing his will.
With Mary and Jesus,
you answer the Holy Spirit's call to build a better world.
With one heart, we join you in saying:
Here we are, Lord, your will be done!
Your kingdom come nearer to us!
Keep the hope of a new world alive in our hearts.
Inspire us to speak words of tenderness to awaken
the love of hearts.
May we draw the energy for our actions from the source
of all Love so our faces may shine with the freedom
of the children of God.
Amen.

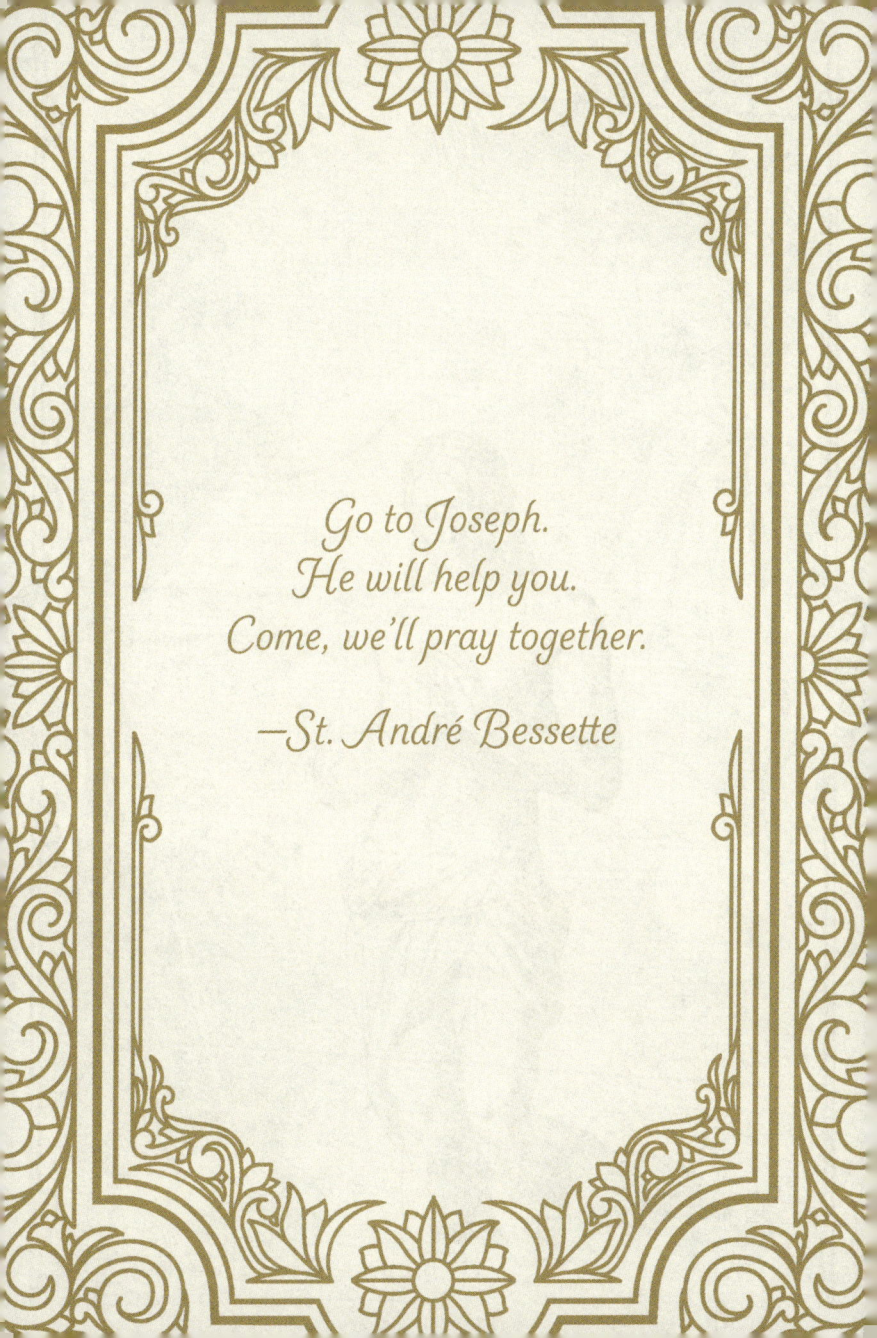

*Go to Joseph.
He will help you.
Come, we'll pray together.*

—St. André Bessette

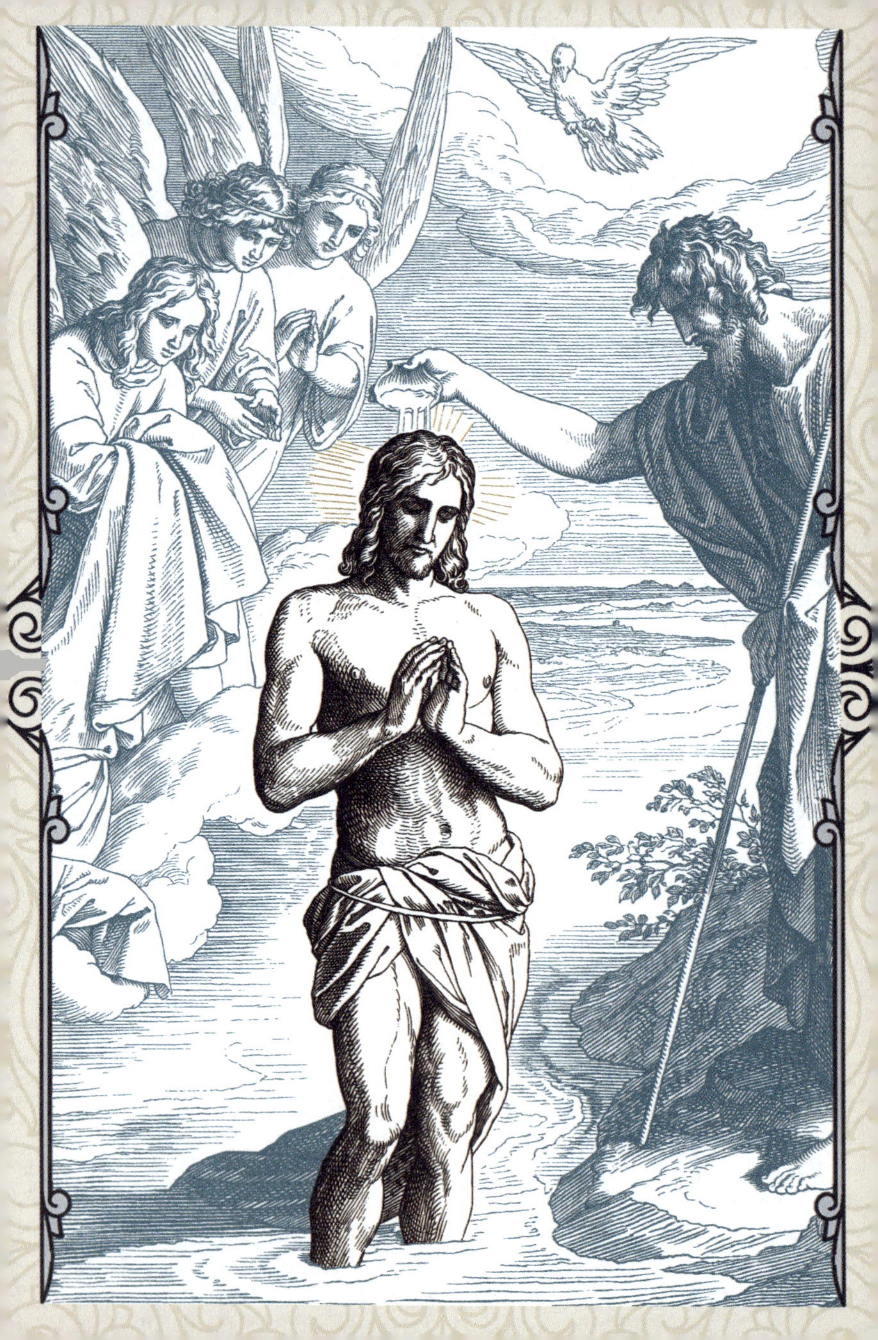

# Prayers of Blessing

The door of heaven is open to all.
Jesus, Jesus, Jesus.
—St. Anna Wang, martyr

| | | |
|---|---|---|
| 89. | Prayer of Blessing to Be Used in Various Circumstances | 133 |
| 90. | Blessing of a Family | 135 |
| 91. | Blessing of a Married Couple | 136 |
| 92. | Blessing of Children | 138 |
| 93. | Blessing of a New Home | 140 |
| 94. | Blessing of Homes during the Christmas and Easter Seasons | 141 |
| 95. | Blessing on the Anniversary of a Baptism | 142 |
| 96. | Blessing on the Occasion of a Birthday | 143 |

| | |
|---|---|
| 97. Godparent's Blessing of a Child | 144 |
| 98. Blessing of an Engaged Couple | 145 |
| 99. Blessing of the Sick | 146 |
| 100. Blessing of a Person Suffering from Addiction | 147 |
| 101. Blessing of the Elderly | 148 |
| 102. Blessing of Those Who Are Homebound | 149 |
| 103. Prayer with the Dying | 150 |
| 104. Prayer for the Dead | 151 |

# Prayer of Blessing to Be Used in Various Circumstances

### Blessing of natural products:

>Blessed are you, O God,
>Creator of the universe,
>who have made all things good
>and given the earth for us to cultivate.
>Grant that we may always use created things gratefully
>and share your gifts with those in need,
>out of love for Christ our Lord,
>who lives and reigns with you for ever and ever.
>R. Amen.

### Blessing of manufactured things:

>Almighty and ever-living God,
>you made us stewards over the created world,
>so that in all things we might honor the demands of charity.
>Graciously hear our prayers,
>that your blessing may come upon all those who use these objects for their needs.

Let them always see you as the good surpass-
 ing every good
and love their neighbor with upright hearts.
We ask this through Christ our Lord.
R. Amen.

*Blessing for the special occasions of life:*

Lord God,
from the abundance of your mercy
enrich your servants and safeguard them.
Strengthened by your blessing,
may they always be thankful to you
and bless you with unending joy.
We ask this through Christ our Lord.
R. Amen.

# Blessing of a Family

We bless your name, O Lord,
for sending your own incarnate Son,
to become part of a family,
so that, as he lived its life,
he would experience its worries and its joys.
We ask you, Lord,
to protect and watch over this family,
so that in the strength of your grace
its members may enjoy prosperity,
possess the priceless gift of your peace,
and, as the Church alive in the home,
bear witness in this world to your glory.
We ask this through Christ our Lord.
R. Amen.

# Blessing of a Married Couple

*On the 25th, 50th, 60th, or other anniversary:*

Lord God and Creator,
we bless and praise your name.
In the beginning you made man and woman,
so that they might enter a communion of life and love.
You likewise blessed the union of *N.* with *N.*,
so that they might reflect the union of Christ with his Church:
look with kindness on them today.
Amid the joys and struggles of their life
you have preserved the union between them;
renew their marriage covenant,
increase your love in them,
and strengthen their bond of peace,
so that (surrounded by their children)
they may always rejoice in the gift of your blessing.
We ask this through Christ our Lord.
R. Amen.

*On other occasions:*

> Almighty and eternal God,
> you have so exalted the unbreakable bond
>     of marriage
> that it has become the sacramental sign
> of your Son's union with the Church as his
>     spouse.
>
> Look with favor on N. and N.,
> whom you have united in marriage,
> as they ask for your help
> and the protection of the Virgin Mary.
> They pray that in good times and in bad
> they will grow in love for each other;
> that they will resolve to be of one heart in
>     the bond of peace.
> Lord, in their struggles let them rejoice
> that you are near to help them;
> in their needs let them know
> that you are there to rescue them;
> in their joys let them see
> that you are the source and completion of
>     every happiness.
> We ask this through Christ our Lord.
> R. Amen.

# Blessing of Children

*For a child already baptized:*

Lord Jesus Christ,
you loved children so much that you said:
"Whoever welcomes a child welcomes me."
Hear our prayers and,
with your unfailing protection,
watch over this child
whom you have blessed with the grace of baptism.
When he/she has grown to maturity,
grant that he/she will confess your name in willing faith,
be fervent in charity,
and persevere courageously in the hope of reaching your kingdom,
where you live and reign for ever and ever.
R. Amen.

*For a child not yet baptized:*

> All-powerful God and Father,
> you are the source of all blessings,
> the protector of infants,
> whose gift of children
> enriches and brightens a marriage.
> Look with favor on this child and,
> when he/she is reborn of water and the
>   Holy Spirit,
> bring him/her into your own spiritual family,
>   the Church,
> there to become a sharer in your kingdom
> and with us to bless your name for ever.
> We ask this through Christ our Lord.
> R. Amen.

# Blessing of a New Home

Lord,
be close to your servants
who move into this home
and ask for your blessing.
Be their shelter when they are at home,
their companion when they are away,
and their welcome guest when they return.
And at last receive them
into the dwelling place you have prepared
    for them
in your Father's house,
where you live for ever and ever.

# Blessing of Homes during the Christmas and Easter Seasons

*For the Christmas season:*

>Lord God of heaven and earth,
>you revealed your only-begotten Son to every nation
>by the guidance of a star.
>Bless this house and all who inhabit it.
>Fill them with the light of Christ,
>that their concern for others may reflect your love.
>We ask this through Christ our Lord.
>R. Amen.

*For the Easter season:*

>Lord,
>we rejoice in the victory of your Son over death:
>by rising from the tomb to new life
>he gives us new hope and promise.
>Bless all the members of this household
>and surround them with your protection,
>that they may find comfort and peace
>in Jesus Christ, the paschal lamb,

who lives and reigns with you and the Holy
> Spirit,
one God, for ever and ever.
R. Amen.

# Blessing on the Anniversary of a Baptism

N., on this day the Christian community
welcomed you with great joy.
You were baptized in the name of the Father,
and of the Son, and of the Holy Spirit.
You put on the Lord Jesus.
Today we sign you again with the cross
by which you were claimed for Christ,
and we pray that God's blessing be upon
> you.

*Each person signs the forehead of the one celebrating the anniversary and says:*
Blessed be God who chose you in Christ.

# Blessing on the Occasion of a Birthday

## For adults:

> God of all creation,
> we offer you grateful praise for the gift of life.
> Hear the prayers of N., your servant,
> who recalls today the day of his/her birth
> and rejoices in your gifts
> of life and love, family and friends.
> Bless him/her with your presence
> and surround him/her with your love
> that he/she may enjoy many happy years,
> all of them pleasing to you.
> We ask this through Christ our Lord.
> R. Amen.

## For children:

> Loving God,
> you created all the people of the world
> and you know each of us by name.
> We thank you for N.,
> who today celebrates his/her birthday.
> Bless him/her with your love and friendship
> that he/she may grow in wisdom,

knowledge, and grace.
May he/she love his/her family always
and be faithful to his/her friends.
Grant this through Christ our Lord.
R. Amen.

# Godparent's Blessing of a Child

*N.*, blessed be God who chose you in Christ.
*N.*, may Christ's peace reign in your heart.

# Blessing of an Engaged Couple

We praise you, Lord,
for your gentle plan draws together your
    children, *N.* and *N.*,
in love for one another.
Strengthen their hearts,
so that they will keep faith with each other,
please you in all things,
and so come to the happiness of celebrating
    the sacrament of their marriage.
We ask this through Christ our Lord.
R. Amen.

# Blessing of the Sick

Lord and Father,
almighty and eternal God,
by your blessing
you give us strength and support in our frailty:
turn with kindness toward your servant, *N*.
Free him/her from all illness
and restore him/her to health,
so that in the sure knowledge of your goodness
he/she will gratefully bless your holy name.
We ask this through Christ our Lord.
R. Amen.

# Blessing of a Person Suffering from Addiction

God of mercy,
we bless you in the name of your Son, Jesus
    Christ,
who ministered to all who came to him.
Give your strength to *N.*, your servant,
enfold him/her in your love
and restore him/her to the freedom of God's
    children.

Lord,
look with compassion on all those
who have lost their health and freedom.
Restore to them the assurance of your
    unfailing mercy,
strengthen them in the work of recovery,
and help them to resist all temptation.
To those who care for them,
grant patient understanding and a love that
    perseveres.
We ask this through Christ our Lord.
R. Amen.

# Blessing of the Elderly

Lord God almighty, bless your servant, *N*., to
   whom you have given a long life.
Let him/her be aware of your nearness,
so that, when he/she worries about past
   failings,
he/she will rejoice in your mercy and,
when he/she thinks of the future,
he/she will faithfully rely on you as his/her
   hope.
We ask this through Christ our Lord.
R. Amen.

# Blessing of Those Who Are Homebound

Lord, our God,
you have given these your faithful
the grace to maintain their hope in you
through all life's changes
and to taste and see your goodness.
We bless you for the gifts you have showered
 on them.
We ask that they may find joy in a renewed
 strength of spirit,
that they may have good health,
and that they may inspire us by the example
 of their serene way of life.
We ask this through Christ our Lord.
R. Amen.

# Prayer with the Dying

Go forth, Christian soul, from this world
in the name of God the almighty Father,
who created you,
in the name of Jesus Christ, Son of the living
    God,
who suffered for you,
in the name of the Holy Spirit,
who was poured out upon you,
go forth, faithful Christian.

May you live in peace this day,
may your home be with God in Zion,
with Mary, the Virgin Mother of God,
with Joseph, and all the angels and saints.

# Prayer for the Dead

Into your hands, O Lord,
we humbly entrust our brothers and sisters.
In this life you embraced them with your
 tender love;
deliver them now from every evil
and bid them enter eternal rest.

The old order has passed away:
welcome them into paradise,
where there will be no sorrow,
no weeping nor pain,
but fullness of peace and joy
with your Son and the Holy Spirit
forever and ever.
R. Amen.

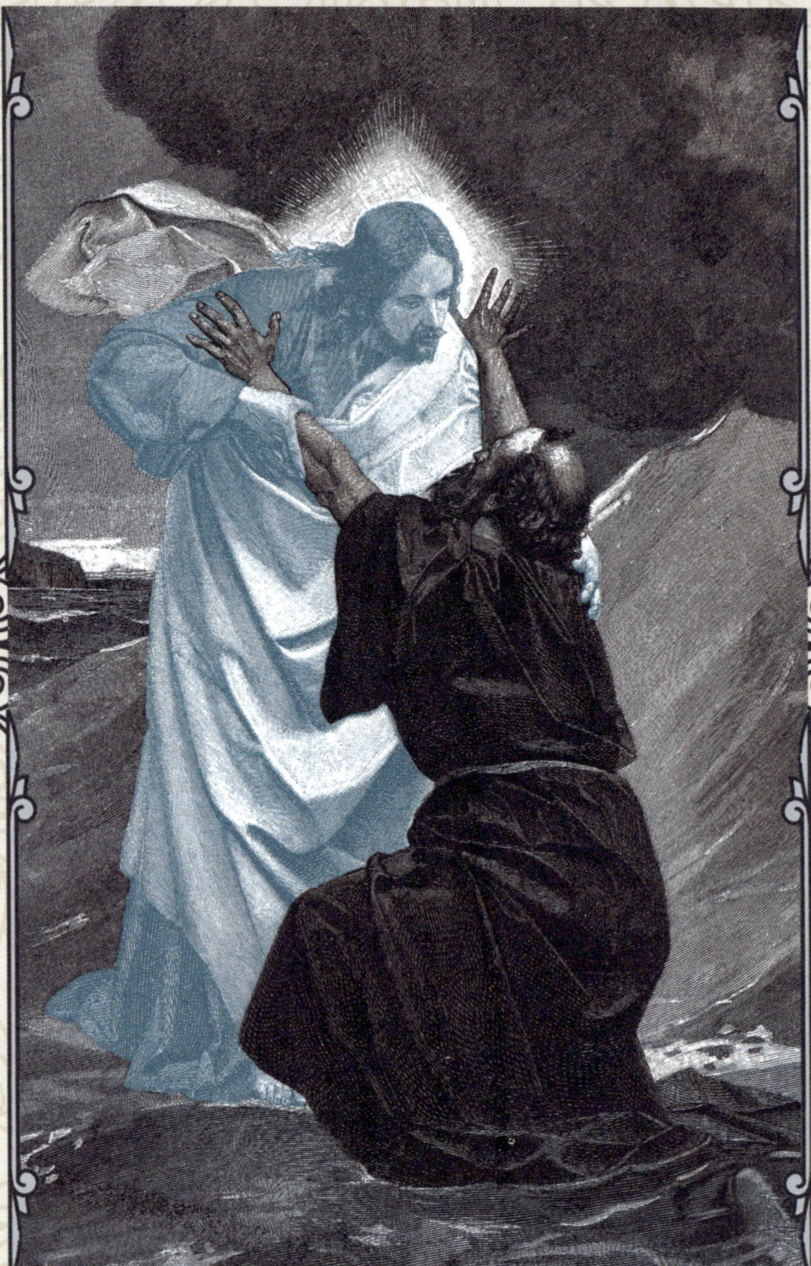

# Petitionary Prayers: Drawing Close to the Lord in Times of Need

Pray and God will do the rest.
—St. Josephine Bakhita

| | | |
|---|---|---|
| 105. | Abba, Father—Mark 14:36 | 155 |
| 106. | Grant Me the Favor I Implore—St. John Eudes | 155 |
| 107. | Prayer of St. Elizabeth Ann Seton | 156 |
| 108. | Thank You, Lord Jesus Christ—St. Richard of Chichester | 157 |

| | |
|---|---|
| 109. God of Life—St. Augustine | 158 |
| 110. Bookmark of St. Teresa of Avila | 159 |

## Abba, Father

*This was the prayer of Jesus in the Garden of Gethsemane: dreading what was ahead, yet trusting in the goodness of his Father's plan.*

> Abba, Father, all things are possible to you;
> remove this chalice from me; yet not what I
> will, but what you will.
>
> Mark 14:36

## Grant Me the Favor I Implore

> O desire of my soul, grant me the favor I
>     implore;
> hearken to the cry of my heart.
> You know, O Lord, what I ask of you;
> My heart has so often told you.
>
> St. John Eudes

# Prayer of St. Elizabeth Ann Seton

Lord Jesus, who was born for us in a stable,
lived for us a life of pain and sorrow,
and died for us upon a cross;
say for us in the hour of death, *Father, forgive*,
and to Your Mother, *Behold your child*.
Say to us, *This day you shall be with Me in paradise*.
Dear Savior, leave us not, forsake us not.
We thirst for You, Fountain of Living Water.
Our days pass quickly along, soon all will be consummated for us.
To Your hands we commend our spirits, now and forever.
Amen.

St. Elizabeth Ann Seton

# Thank You, Lord Jesus Christ

Thank you, Lord Jesus Christ,
For all the benefits and blessings
Which you have given me,
For all the pains and insults
Which you have borne for me.
Merciful Friend, Brother and Redeemer,
May I know you more clearly,
Love you more clearly,
And follow you more nearly,
Day by day.

St. Richard of Chichester

# God of Life

God of life, there are days when the burdens we carry
chafe our shoulders and wear us down;
when the road seems dreary and endless, the skies gray and threatening;
when our lives have no music in them and our hearts are lonely,
and our souls have lost their courage.
Flood the path with light, we beseech you;
turn our eyes to where the skies are full of promise.

St. Augustine

# Bookmark of St. Teresa of Avila

Let nothing disturb you,
nothing frighten you,
all things are passing;
Patient endurance
attains all things:
one whom God possesses wants nothing
for God alone suffices.

St. Teresa of Avila

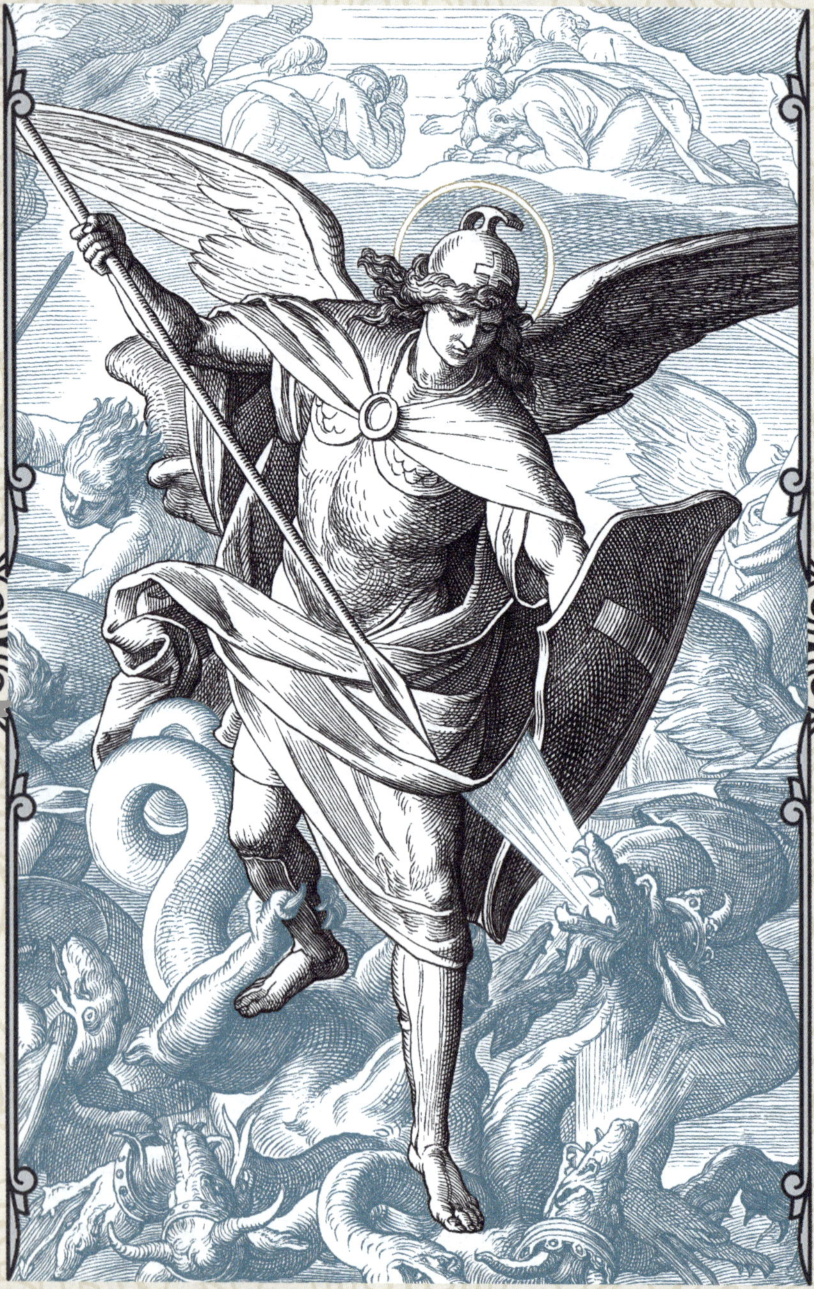

# Prayers for Deliverance

> I am dust and ashes; for that reason, I place no bounds in my petition for mercy; for that reason, I have confidence; for that reason, I have hope; for that reason, I dare to ask the Lord even for "the kiss of His mouth," as the spouse in the Canticle of Canticles.
>
> —Servant of God
> Archbishop Luis Maria Martinez

| | |
|---|---|
| 111. St. Michael the Archangel | 162 |
| 112. Lord, I Cannot Do This Unless You Enable Me—Br. Lawrence | 162 |
| 113. The Dragon Is Here Again—St. Gregory Nanzianzus | 163 |
| 114. Prayer for Times of Illness—St. John Bosco | 163 |

## St. Michael the Archangel

St. Michael the Archangel, defend us in battle.
Be our protection against the wickedness and snares of the devil.
May God rebuke him, we humbly pray;
and do thou, O Prince of the Heavenly Host,
by the power of God, thrust into hell Satan and all evil spirits
who wander through the world for the ruin of souls.
Amen.

## Lord, I Cannot Do This Unless You Enable Me

Lord, I cannot do this unless you enable me.
Br. Lawrence

## The Dragon Is Here Again

Alas, dear Christ, the Dragon is here again.
Alas, he is here: terror has seized me, and fear.
Alas that I ate of the fruit of the tree of knowledge.
Alas that his envy led me to envy too.
I did not become like God; I was cast out of Paradise.
Temper, sword, awhile, the heat of your flames
and let me go again about the garden,
entering with Christ, a thief from another tree.

St. Gregory Nazianzus

## Prayer for Times of Illness

Yes, Lord, if it please you, cure me. I will not refuse any work. If I can be of service to a few souls, grant, O Lord, by the intercession of your most holy Mother, to return me to such health as will not be contrary to the welfare of my soul.

St. John Bosco

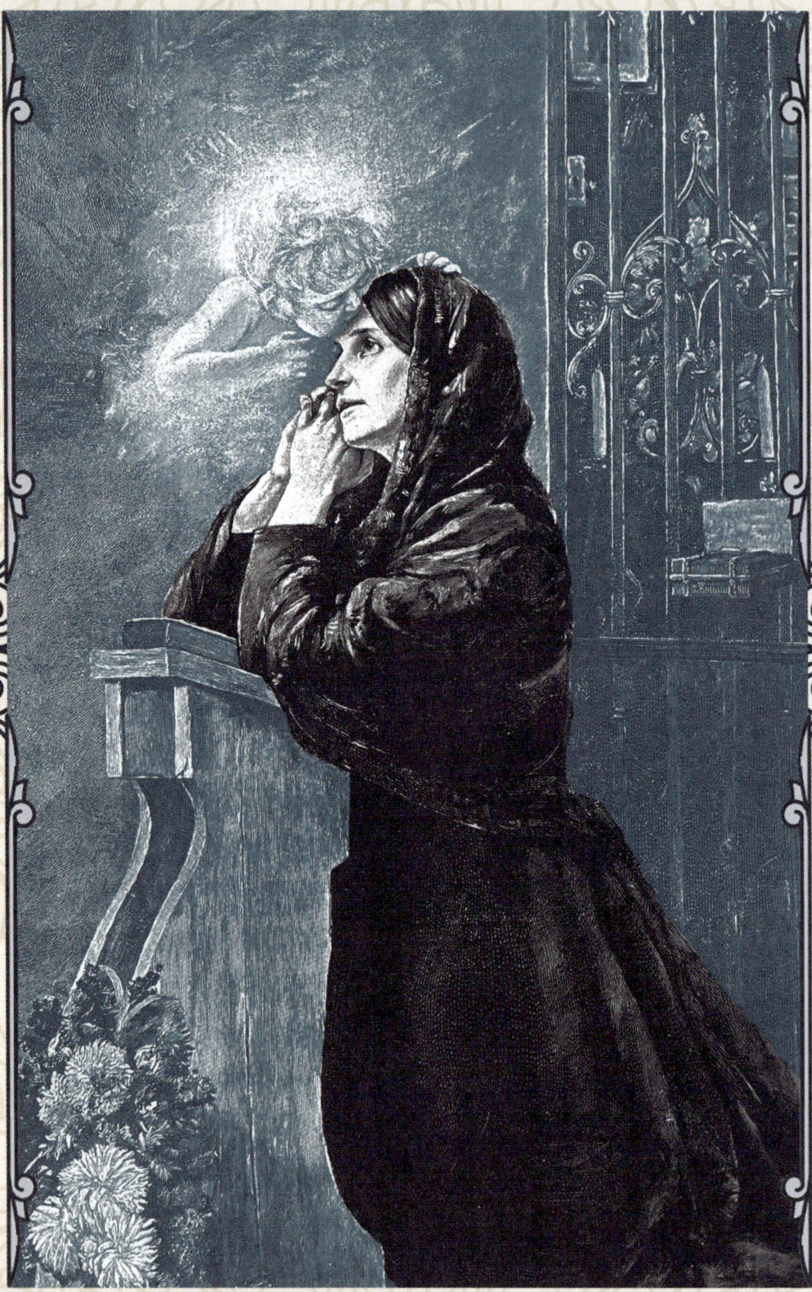

# Prayers for Special Graces

> My prayer is but a cold affair, Lord, because my love burns with so small a flame, but you who are rich in mercy will not mete out to them your gifts according to the dullness of my zeal, but as your kindness is above all human love so let your eagerness to hear be greater than the feeling in my prayers.
>
> —St. Anselm

| | |
|---|---|
| 115. Serenity Prayer—Attributed to Reinhold Niebuhr | 167 |
| 116. Litany of Humility—Rafael Cardinal Merry del Val y Zulueta | 168 |
| 117. Litany of Trust—Sr. Faustina Maria Pia | 171 |

118. Prayer of Trust and Confidence—
St. Padre Pio 174
119. Although My Frailty Is Great—
Servant of God Archbishop Luis Maria
Martinez 175
120. Into Your Hands—
Servant of God Archbishop Luis Maria
Martinez 176

# Serenity Prayer

God, grant me the serenity
to accept the things I cannot change,
the courage to change the things I can,
and the wisdom to know the difference.
Living one day at a time,
enjoying one moment at a time.
Accepting hardships as the pathway to
  peace.
Taking, as He did, the sinful world as it is,
not as I would have it.
Trusting that He will make all things right
if I surrender to His will;
that I may be reasonably happy in this life,
and supremely happy with Him forever.
                    Attributed to Reinhold Niebuhr

# Litany of Humility

O Jesus, meek and humble of heart, *hear me.*

From the desire of being esteemed, *deliver me, O Jesus.*

From the desire of being loved, *deliver me, O Jesus.*

From the desire of being extolled, *deliver me, O Jesus.*

From the desire of being honored, *deliver me, O Jesus.*

From the desire of being praised, *deliver me, O Jesus.*

From the desire of being preferred to others, *deliver me, O Jesus.*

From the desire of being consulted, *deliver me, O Jesus.*

From the desire of being approved, *deliver me, O Jesus.*

From the fear of being humiliated, *deliver me, O Jesus.*

From the fear of being despised, *deliver me, O Jesus.*

From the fear of suffering rebukes, *deliver me, O Jesus.*

From the fear of being calumniated, *deliver me, O Jesus.*

From the fear of being forgotten, *deliver me, O Jesus.*

From the fear of being ridiculed, *deliver me, O Jesus.*

From the fear of being wronged, *deliver me, O Jesus.*

From the fear of being suspected, *deliver me, O Jesus.*

That others may be loved more than I,
*Jesus, grant me the grace to desire it.*

That others may be esteemed more than I,
*Jesus, grant me the grace to desire it.*

That, in the opinion of the world, others may increase and I may decrease,
*Jesus, grant me the grace to desire it.*

That others may be chosen and I set aside,
*Jesus, grant me the grace to desire it.*

That others may be praised and I go unnoticed,
*Jesus, grant me the grace to desire it.*

That others may be preferred to me in everything,
*Jesus, grant me the grace to desire it.*

That others may become holier than I, provided that I may become as holy as I should,
*Jesus, grant me the grace to desire it.*
Cardinal Rafael Merry del Val y Zulueta

# Litany of Trust

From the belief that I have to earn your love, *deliver me, Jesus.*

From the fear that I am unlovable, *deliver me, Jesus.*

From the false security that I have what it takes, *deliver me, Jesus.*

From the fear that trusting you will leave me more destitute, *deliver me, Jesus.*

From all suspicion of your words and promises, *deliver me, Jesus.*

From the rebellion against childlike dependency on you, *deliver me, Jesus.*

From refusals and reluctances in accepting your will, *deliver me, Jesus.*

From anxiety about the future, *deliver me, Jesus.*

From resentment or excessive preoccupation with the past, *deliver me, Jesus.*

From restless self-seeking in the present moment, *deliver me, Jesus.*

From disbelief in your love and presence, *deliver me, Jesus.*

From the fear of being asked to give more than I have, *deliver me, Jesus.*

From the belief that my life has no meaning or worth, *deliver me, Jesus.*
From the fear of what love demands, *deliver me, Jesus.*
From discouragement, *deliver me, Jesus.*
That you are continually holding me, sustaining me, loving me,
*Jesus, I trust in you.*
That your love goes deeper than my sins and failings and transforms me,
*Jesus, I trust in you.*
That not knowing what tomorrow brings is an invitation to lean on you,
*Jesus, I trust in you.*
That you are with me in my suffering,
*Jesus, I trust in you.*
That my suffering, united to your own, will bear fruit in this life and the next,
*Jesus, I trust in you.*
That you will not leave me orphan, that you are present in your Church,
*Jesus, I trust in you.*
That your plan is better than anything else,
*Jesus, I trust in you.*
That you always hear me and in your goodness always respond to me,
*Jesus, I trust in you.*

That you give me the grace to accept forgiveness and to forgive others,
*Jesus, I trust in you.*
That you give me all the strength I need for what is asked,
*Jesus, I trust in you.*
That my life is a gift,
*Jesus, I trust in you.*
That you will teach me to trust you,
*Jesus, I trust in you.*
That you are my Lord and my God,
*Jesus, I trust in you.*
That I am your beloved one,
*Jesus, I trust in you.*

Sr. Faustina Maria Pia

# Prayer of Trust and Confidence

O Lord, we ask for a boundless confidence and trust in your divine mercy, and the courage to accept the crosses and sufferings which bring immense goodness to our souls and that of your Church.

Help us to love you with a pure and contrite heart, and to humble ourselves beneath your cross, as we climb the mountain of holiness, carrying our cross that leads to heavenly glory. May we receive you with great faith and love in Holy Communion, and allow you to act in us, as you desire, for your greater glory.

O Jesus, most adorable heart and eternal fountain of Divine Love, may our prayer find favor before the Divine Majesty of Your Heavenly Father. Amen.

St. Padre Pio

# Although My Frailty Is Great

Although my frailty is great and my amazing gift of liberty may snatch me from God's arms to cast me down the slope that leads to the abyss, I know that God loves me sufficiently either not to allow this or, if he should permit it, to come to look for me. He will descend with his love and his omnipotence along the slope that leads to destruction and he will take me in his arms, and like a good shepherd, he will place me upon his shoulders and bring me back to the fold. No, I do not fear my weakness, for as St. Thérèse of the Child Jesus said, "I know upon what I am relying in the love and the mercy of my Savior."

Servant of God
Archbishop Luis Maria Martinez

# Into Your Hands

Lord, into your hands I place both my will and my fidelity. I hope from you not only your promised graces but also the will which that promise includes.

>Servant of God
>Archbishop Luis Maria Martinez

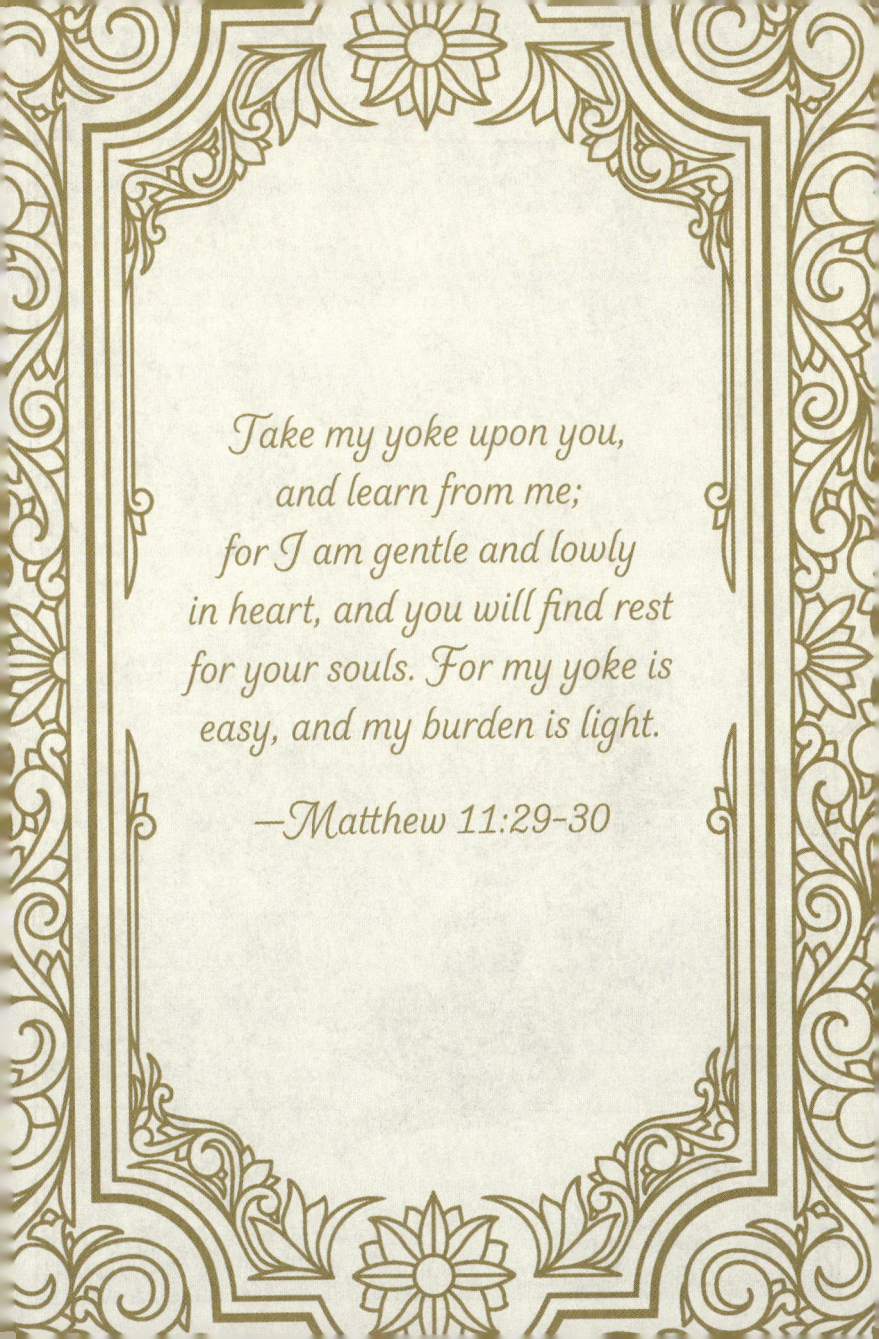

*Take my yoke upon you,
and learn from me;
for I am gentle and lowly
in heart, and you will find rest
for your souls. For my yoke is
easy, and my burden is light.*

—Matthew 11:29-30

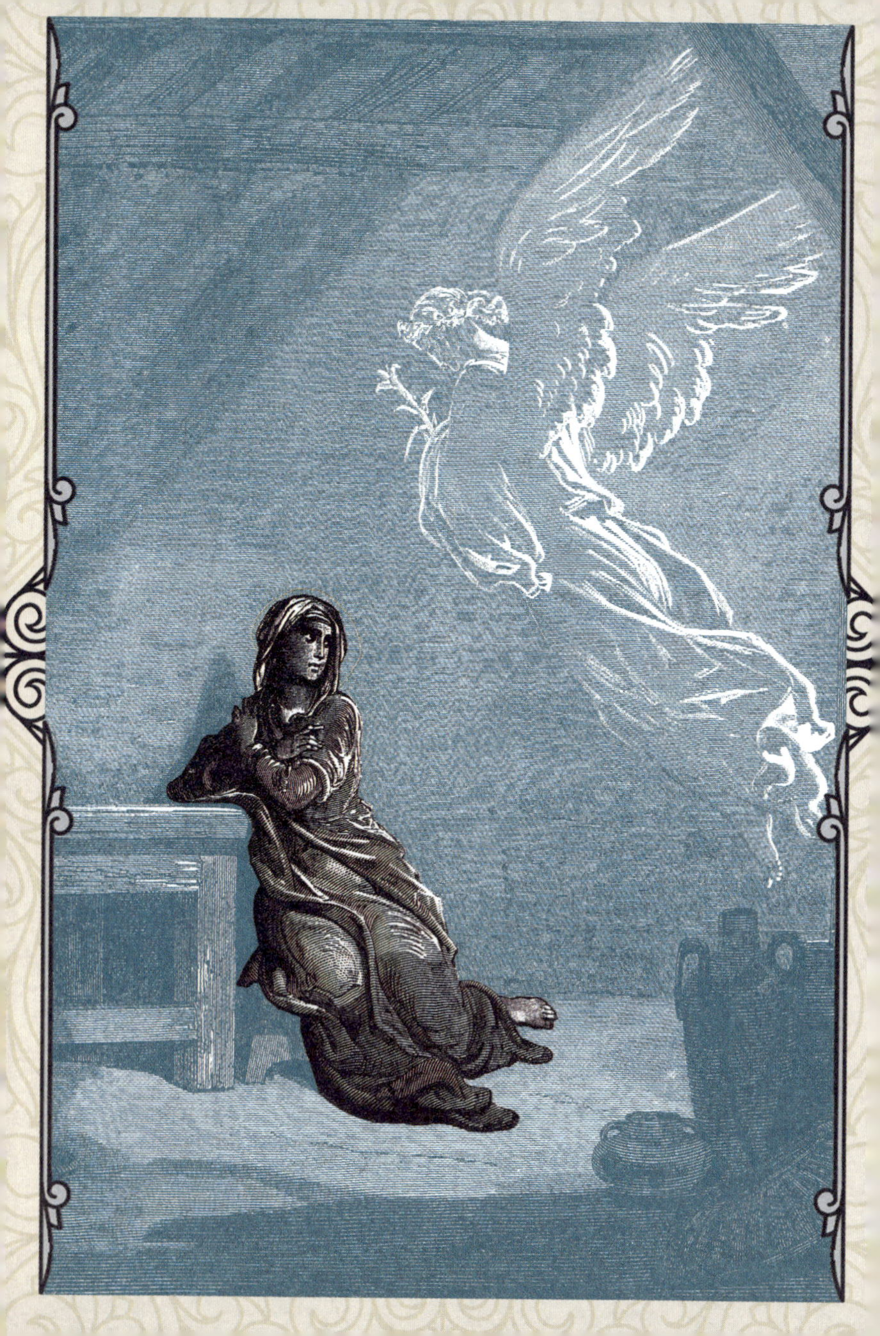

# Prayers of Surrender to God's Loving Will

*Not as I will, but as you will.*
—Matthew 26:39

| | |
|---|---|
| 121. If You Want It, I Want It Too—<br>Bl. Chiara Badano | 180 |
| 122. O Jesus, I Surrender Myself to You—<br>Fr. Dolindo Ruotolo | 180 |
| 123. Lord, Give Me the Grace to Welcome the Grace—<br>Servant of God Chiara Corbella Petrillo | 181 |
| 124. Prayer for Generosity—<br>St. Ignatius of Loyola | 181 |

## If You Want It, I Want It Too

For you, Jesus. If you want it, I want it too.
>Bl. Chiara Badano

## O Jesus, I Surrender Myself to You

O Jesus, I surrender myself to you, take care of everything!
>Fr. Dolindo Ruotolo

# Lord, Give Me the Grace to Welcome the Grace

Lord, give me the grace to welcome the grace.

Servant of God<br>Chiara Corbella Petrillo

# Prayer for Generosity

Dearest Lord, teach me to be generous.
Teach me to serve as you deserve;
to give and not to count the cost;
to fight and not to heed the wounds;
to labor and not to seek to rest;
to give of myself and not to ask for reward,
except the reward of knowing that I am
    doing your will.

St. Ignatius of Loyola

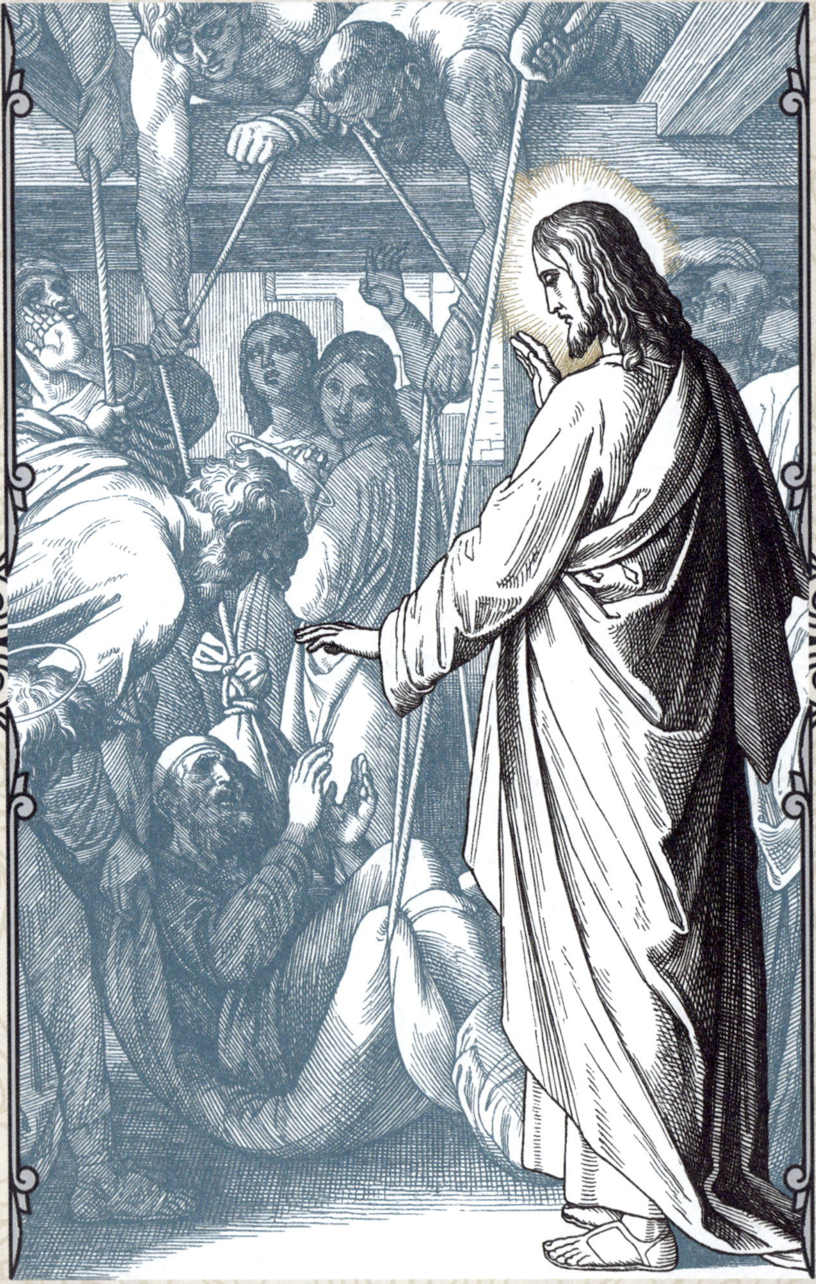

# Prayers for the Grace of Forgiveness

*All shall be well, and all shall be well, and all manner of things shall be well.*
—St. Julian of Norwich

125. Prayer for Understanding—
    Adapted from the Novena for Forgiveness
    to St. Josemaría Escrivá                184

126. Prayer Asking for Mary's Help Forgiving Another—
    Adapted from the Novena for Forgiveness
    to St. Josemaría Escrivá                185

## Prayer for Understanding

Jesus, you see how difficult I find it to understand others, to see the best in them and forgive their faults when they upset me and hurt me. I ask you for the grace to fulfill your command: "Judge not, and you will not be judged; condemn not, and you will not be condemned; forgive, and you will be forgiven" (Luke 6:37).

You know, Lord, that often the first thing I notice about people is the negative things, the things that annoy me, that I see as ridiculous or unbearable. And so I develop the vice of thinking and speaking badly about others.

Lord, have mercy on me, who am so unmerciful. Although I don't deserve it, I beg you to grant me . . . a heart that is able to understand and forgive.

Adapted from the<br>Novena for Forgiveness to<br>St. Josemaría Escrivá

# Prayer Asking for Mary's Help Forgiving Another

Mother of Mercy, Comforter of the afflicted, Refuge of sinners, you were united to the sacrifice of Jesus when he shed his Blood on the Cross to cleanse us from our sins: take pity on us poor sinners, when we cannot manage to forgive.

When we feel resentment, anger, or the desire for revenge burning inside us, make us remember you. Never let us forget that we have a Mother who loves us and who wants to soften our hard hearts with the warmth of her Immaculate Heart.

Enfold us, Mother, in your embrace like small children; calm our anger with your smile; obtain for us from your Son the gift of forgiving, forgetting, and not stirring up grudges; and also of loving and wishing well those who do not wish us well. Lead us, Mother . . . deep into the Sacred and Merciful Heart of Jesus.

Adapted from the<br>Novena for Forgiveness to<br>St. Josemaría Escrivá

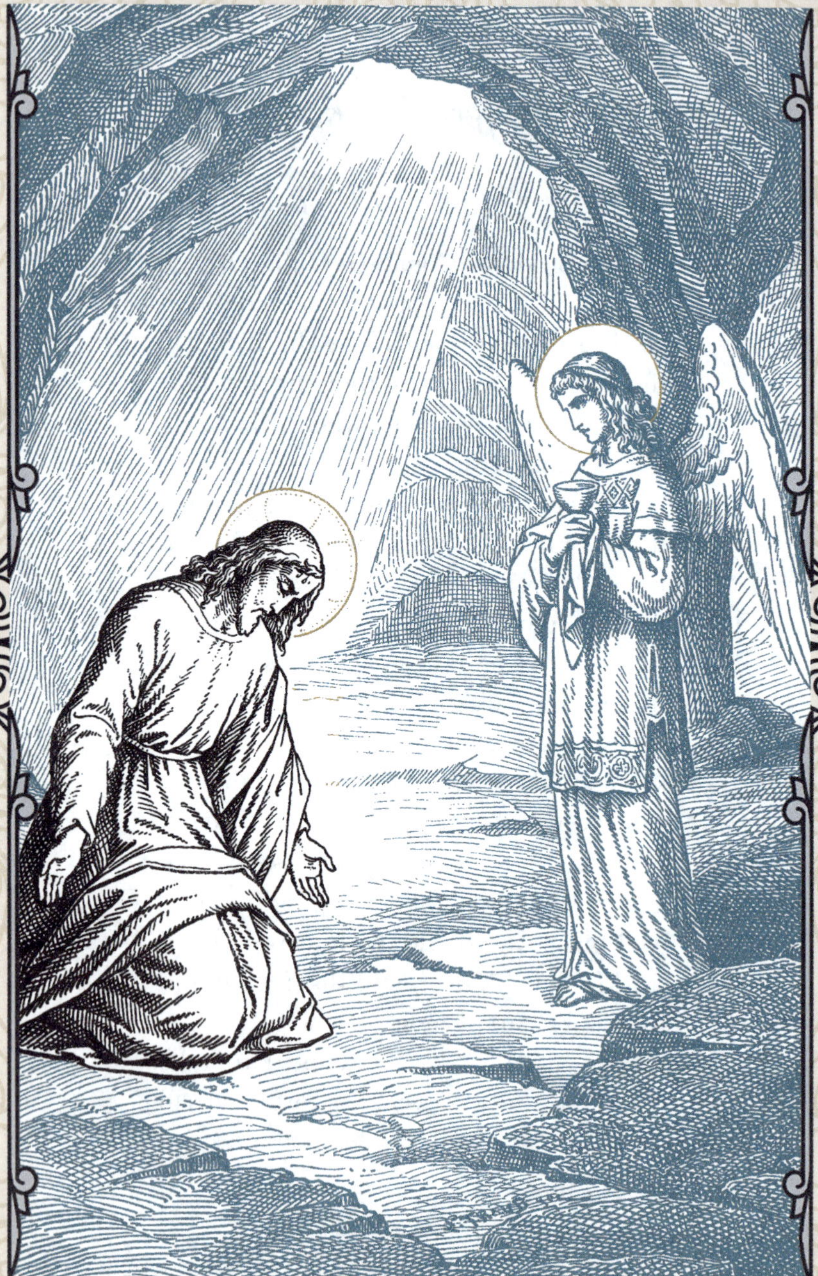

# Intercessory Prayers

It helps, now and then, to step back and take a long view. . . . We accomplish in our lifetime only a tiny fraction of the magnificent enterprise that is God's work. Nothing we do is complete . . . the Kingdom always lies beyond us. No statement says all that could be said. No prayer fully expresses our faith. . . . We cannot do everything, and there is a sense of liberation in realizing that. This enables us to do something, and to do it very well. It may be incomplete, but it is a beginning, a step along the way, an opportunity for the Lord's grace to enter and do the rest. We may never see the end results, but that is the difference between the master builder and the worker. We are workers, not master builders; ministers, not messiahs. We are prophets of a future not our own.

—Bishop Ken Untener

| | |
|---|---|
| 127. Grant Us Your Help and Protection—St. Clement of Rome | 190 |
| 128. Prayer for Marriage and Families—St. John Paul II | 191 |
| 129. Prayer for Christian Unity | 192 |
| 130. Prayer for the Church through Mary's Intercession—St. John Paul II | 193 |
| 131. Prayer for Vocations—St. Paul VI | 194 |
| 132. Prayer for Seminarians—St. Thérèse of Lisieux | 195 |
| 133. Prayer for Priests—Pope Benedict XVI | 196 |
| 134. Prayer for Priests through Mary's Intercession—Attributed to St. Teresa of Calcutta | 197 |
| 135. Prayer for Souls—St. Gertrude | 198 |
| 136. Prayer for Our Country—Servant of God Theotonius Amal Ganguly | 199 |
| 137. Prayer for Peace—Pope Francis | 200 |
| 138. Prayer for Marginalized Persons | 202 |
| 139. Prayer to Cooperate with the Holy Spirit's Movement in the World—Servant of God Thea Bowman | 204 |

| | |
|---|---|
| 140. Prayer for Breaking Racial and Social Barriers—Servant of God Thea Bowman | 205 |
| 141. Prayer for Healing for Victims of Abuse | 206 |
| 142. Prayer for Community | 208 |
| 143. Prayer for the Life and Dignity of the Human Person | 209 |
| 144. Prayer to End Abortion—Priests for Life | 210 |
| 145. Prayer for Migrants and Refugees—Pope Francis | 212 |
| 146. Prayer to Care for Our Common Home—Pope Francis | 213 |

# Grant Us Your Help and Protection

We beseech you, O Lord, to grant us your help and protection. Deliver the afflicted, pity the lowly, raise the fallen, reveal yourself to the needy, heal the sick, and bring home your wandering people. Feed the hungry, ransom the captive, support the weak, comfort the fainthearted. Let all the nations of the earth know that you alone are God, that Jesus Christ is your child, and that we are your people and the sheep of your pasture.

St. Clement of Rome

# Prayer for Marriage and Families

Lord God, from you every family in heaven and on earth takes its name.

Father, you are Love and Life.

Through your Son, Jesus Christ, born of woman, and through the Holy Spirit, fountain of divine charity, grant that every family on earth may become for each successive generation a true shrine of life and love.

Grant that your grace may guide the thoughts and actions of husbands and wives for the good of their families and of all the families in the world.

Grant that the young may find in the family solid support for their human dignity and for their growth in truth and love.

Grant that love, strengthened by the grace of the sacrament of marriage, may prove mightier than all the weakness and trials through which our families sometimes pass.

Through the intercession of the Holy Family of Nazareth, grant that the Church may fruitfully carry out her worldwide mission in the family and through the family.

Through Christ our Lord, who is the Way, the Truth and the Life for ever and ever.

Amen.

St. John Paul II

# Prayer for Christian Unity

Lord Jesus Christ,
You call us together in faith and love.
Breathe again the new life of your Holy
    Spirit among us
that we may hear your holy Word,
pray in your name,
seek unity among Christians,
and live more fully the faith we profess.
All glory and honor be yours
with the Father, and the Holy Spirit, forever
    and ever.
Amen.

# Prayer for the Church through Mary's Intercession

Mother of the Church, grant that the Church may enjoy freedom and peace in fulfilling her saving mission and that to this end she may become mature with a new maturity of faith and inner unity.

Help us to overcome opposition and difficulties. Help us to rediscover all the simplicity and dignity of the Christian vocation. Grant that there may be no lack of "labourers in the Lord's vineyard." Sanctify families. Watch over the souls of the young and the hearts of the children. Help us to overcome the great moral threats against the fundamental spheres of life and love. Obtain for us the grace to be continually renewed through all the beauty of witness given to the Cross and Resurrection of your Son.

St. John Paul II

## Prayer for Vocations

Enlightened and encouraged by your Word, we ask you, Lord, for all those who have already followed and now live your call. For your bishops, priests and deacons; and also for your consecrated religious, brothers and sisters; and also for your missionaries and for the generous lay people who work in the ministries instituted or recognized by the Holy Church. Support them in difficulties, comfort them in suffering, assist them in loneliness, protect them in persecution, confirm them in fidelity!

We ask you, Lord, for those who are opening their souls to your call or are already preparing to follow it. May your Word enlighten them, may your example conquer them, may your grace guide them to the goal of holy orders, religious vows, the missionary mandate.

May your Word, Lord, be a guide and support for all of them so that they know how to guide, advise and support their brothers with that force of conviction and love that You possess and that only You can communicate.

St. Paul VI

## Prayer for Seminarians

Divine Jesus, listen to the prayer I am turning to you for he who wishes to be your missionary: protect him in the midst of dangers in the world; make him feel more and more the nothingness and vanity of fleeting things and happiness in knowing how to despise them for your love. Your sublime apostolate is already exerted over those who surround him: may he be an apostle, worthy of your Sacred Heart.

Oh Mary, sweet Queen of Carmel, I entrust to you the soul of this future priest. Teach him from now with how much love you touched the Divine Child Jesus and how you wrapped him in swaddling clothes so that he one day might go up the Holy Altar and carry the King of Heaven in his hands. I ask you again to always protect him in the shade of your virginal mantle until the happy moment when, on leaving this valley of tears, he will be able to contemplate your splendor and enjoy the fruit of his glorious apostolate for the whole of eternity!

St. Thérèse of Lisieux

## Prayer for Priests

Lord Jesus Christ, eternal High Priest, You offered yourself to the Father on the altar of the Cross and through the outpouring of the Holy Spirit gave Your priestly people a share in Your redeeming sacrifice. Hear our prayer for the sanctification of our priests. Grant that all who are ordained to the ministerial priesthood may be ever more conformed to You, the Divine Master. May they preach the Gospel with pure heart and clear conscience. Let them be shepherds according to Your own Heart, single-minded in service to You and to the Church and shining examples of a holy, simple, and joyful life. Through the prayers of the Blessed Virgin Mary, Your Mother and ours, draw all priests and the flocks entrusted to their care to the fullness of eternal life where You live and reign with the Father and the Holy Spirit, one God, forever and ever.

Pope Benedict XVI

# Prayer for Priests through Mary's Intercession

Mary, Mother of Jesus, throw your mantle of purity over our priests. Protect them, guide them, and keep them in your heart. Be a Mother to them, especially in times of discouragement and loneliness. Love them and keep them belonging completely to Jesus. Like Jesus, they, too, are your sons, so keep their hearts pure and virginal. Keep their minds filled with Jesus, and put Jesus always on their lips, so that he is the one they offer to sinner and to all they meet.

Mary, Mother of Jesus, be their Mother, loving them and bringing them joy. Take special care of sick and dying priests, and the ones most tempted. Remember how they spent their youth and old age, their entire lives serving and giving all to Jesus. Mary, bless them and keep a special place for them in your heart. Give them a piece of your heart, so beautiful and pure and immaculate, so full of love and humility, so that they, too, can grow in the likeness of Christ. Dear

Mary, make them humble like you, and holy like Jesus.

> Attributed to St. Teresa of Calcutta

## *Prayer for Souls*

Eternal Father, I offer Thee the Most Precious Blood of Thy Divine Son, Jesus, in union with all the masses said throughout the world today, for all the holy souls in purgatory, and for sinners everywhere: for sinners in the universal Church, for those in my own home, and for those within my family. Amen.

> St. Gertrude

## Prayer for Our Country

May God bless our country, our leaders, and our people. With them, we shall seek without rest to bring God's blessings to the poor and the hungry and the sick and the needy. May the love of God not be a cloak that hides our laziness or indifference; may the love of neighbor not be an excuse for rashness and impatience. Rather, may love of God and of neighbor be the inspiration that urges us on to greater efforts in the service first of God and then of our fellow men.

Servant of God
Theotonius Amal Ganguly

## Prayer for Peace

Lord God of peace, hear our prayer!

We have tried so many times and over so many years to resolve our conflicts by our own powers and by the force of our arms. How many moments of hostility and darkness have we experienced; how much blood has been shed; how many lives have been shattered; how many hopes have been buried. . . . But our efforts have been in vain.

Now, Lord, come to our aid! Grant us peace, teach us peace; guide our steps in the way of peace. Open our eyes and our hearts, and give us the courage to say: "Never again war!"; "With war everything is lost." Instill in our hearts the courage to take concrete steps to achieve peace.

Lord, God of Abraham, God of the Prophets, God of Love, you created us and you call us to live as brothers and sisters. Give us the strength daily to be instruments of peace; enable us to see everyone who crosses our path as our brother or sister. Make us sensitive to the plea of our citizens who entreat us to turn our weapons of war into implements of peace, our trepidation into confident trust, and our quarreling into forgiveness.

Keep alive within us the flame of hope, so that with patience and perseverance we may opt for dialogue and reconciliation. In this way may peace triumph at last, and may the words "division," "hatred," and "war" be banished from the heart of every man and woman. Lord, defuse the violence of our tongues and our hands. Renew our hearts and minds, so that the word which always brings us together will be "brother," and our way of life will always be that of: Shalom, Peace, Salaam!

Amen.

Pope Francis

## Prayer for Marginalized Persons

For those deprived of their human needs,
and their human rights:
that they may be given the dignity
which God confers on all his people.
We pray to the Lord.

For all who are forgotten or thrown away,
and especially for the poor, the sick, and the
    aged:
that God might change our hearts
and move us to love them as the image of
    Christ.
We pray to the Lord.

For all who are lonely or afraid,
for teenagers on the street,
old people in nursing homes,
prisoners with no one to visit them,
and all whom the world has forgotten:
that Christ might lead us to them.
We pray to the Lord.

For all who are forgotten or cast off:
that we might value each human life,

as a priceless gift from God.
We pray to the Lord.

For those who are mentally disabled:
that we might cherish the gifts God has given them,
and in their lives hear the voice of our loving God.
We pray to the Lord.

# Prayer to Cooperate with the Holy Spirit's Movement in the World

Spirit, touch me.
Touch me with your grace.
Touch me with your wisdom.
Touch me with your love so that I can help somebody,
so that I can serve somebody,
so that I can bless somebody.
Be the bridge over troubled waters
so that I can be the balm in Gilead,
be the hands of Jesus stretched out to heal.

     Servant of God Thea Bowman

# Prayer for Breaking Racial and Social Barriers

Let us be practical, reaching out across the boundaries of race and class and status to help somebody, to encourage and affirm somebody, offering to the young an incentive to learn and grow, offering to the downtrodden resources to help themselves. May our fasting be the kind that saves and shares with the poor, that actually contacts the needy, that gives heart to heart, that touches and nourishes and heals.

Servant of God Thea Bowman

# Prayer for Healing for Victims of Abuse

God of endless love,
ever caring, ever strong,
always present, always just:
You gave your only Son
to save us by the blood of his cross.

Gentle Jesus, shepherd of peace,
join to your own suffering
the pain of all who have been hurt
in body, mind, and spirit
by those who betrayed the trust placed in
 them.

Hear the cries of our brothers and sisters
who have been gravely harmed,
and the cries of those who love them.
Soothe their restless hearts with hope,
steady their shaken spirits with faith.
Grant them justice for their cause,
enlightened by your truth.

Holy Spirit, comforter of hearts,
heal your people's wounds
and transform brokenness into wholeness.

Grant us the courage and wisdom,
humility and grace, to act with justice.
Breathe wisdom into our prayers and labors.
Grant that all harmed by abuse may find
    peace in justice.
We ask this through Christ, our Lord. Amen.

## Prayer for Community

Embracing Father,
You grace each of us with equal measure in
 your love.
Let us learn to love our neighbors more
 deeply,
so that we can create
peaceful and just communities.
Inspire us to use our creative energies
to build the structures we need
to overcome the obstacles
of intolerance and indifference.
May Jesus provide us the example needed
and send the Spirit to warm our hearts for
 the journey.
Amen.

# Prayer for the Life and Dignity of the Human Person

God of all life,
Help us to appreciate the great gift that is human life
formed in your image, a reflection of your holiness.
Help us to recognize you
in all whom you have created:
children not yet born,
families affected by poverty and war,
people of different abilities,
people from other lands, and
all who are victims of hatred and racism.
Help us to bear witness to the dignity of all whom you have created,
regardless of stage of life,
or wealth,
or ability,
or color, or creed,
for every person is fully equal in your loving eyes.
Share with us your holy knowledge
that we are all your children,

each bestowed with inherent dignity.
May your justice reign forever!
Amen.

## *Prayer to End Abortion*

Lord God, I thank you today for the gift of
 my life,
And for the lives of all my brothers and
 sisters.
I know there is nothing that destroys more
 life than abortion,
Yet I rejoice that you have conquered death
By the Resurrection of Your Son.
I am ready to do my part in ending abortion.
Today I commit myself
Never to be silent,
Never to be passive,
Never to be forgetful of the unborn.
I commit myself to be active in the pro-life
 movement,
And never to stop defending life
Until all my brothers and sisters are protected,
And our nation once again becomes
A nation with liberty and justice

Not just for some, but for all,
Through Christ our Lord. Amen!

        Priests for Life

# Prayer for Migrants and Refugees

Lord, make us bearers of hope,
so that where there is darkness,
your light may shine,
and where there is discouragement,
confidence in the future may be reborn.

Lord, make us instruments of your justice,
so that where there is exclusion, fraternity
    may flourish,
and where there is greed, a spirit of sharing
    may grow.

Lord, make us builders of your Kingdom,
together with migrants and refugees
and with all who dwell on the peripheries.

Lord, let us learn how beautiful it is
to live together as brothers and sisters.
Amen.

Pope Francis

# Prayer to Care for Our Common Home

All-powerful God, you are present in the
    whole universe
and in the smallest of your creatures.
You embrace with your tenderness all that
    exists.
Pour out upon us the power of your love,
that we may protect life and beauty.
Fill us with peace, that we may live
as brothers and sisters, harming no one.
O God of the poor,
help us to rescue the abandoned and forgot-
    ten of this earth,
so precious in your eyes.
Bring healing to our lives,
that we may protect the world and not prey
    on it,
that we may sow beauty, not pollution and
    destruction.
Touch the hearts
of those who look only for gain
at the expense of the poor and the earth.
Teach us to discover the worth of each thing,
to be filled with awe and contemplation,

to recognize that we are profoundly united
with every creature as we journey toward
    your infinite light.
We thank you for being with us each day.
Encourage us, we pray, in our struggle
for justice, love, and peace.

Pope Francis

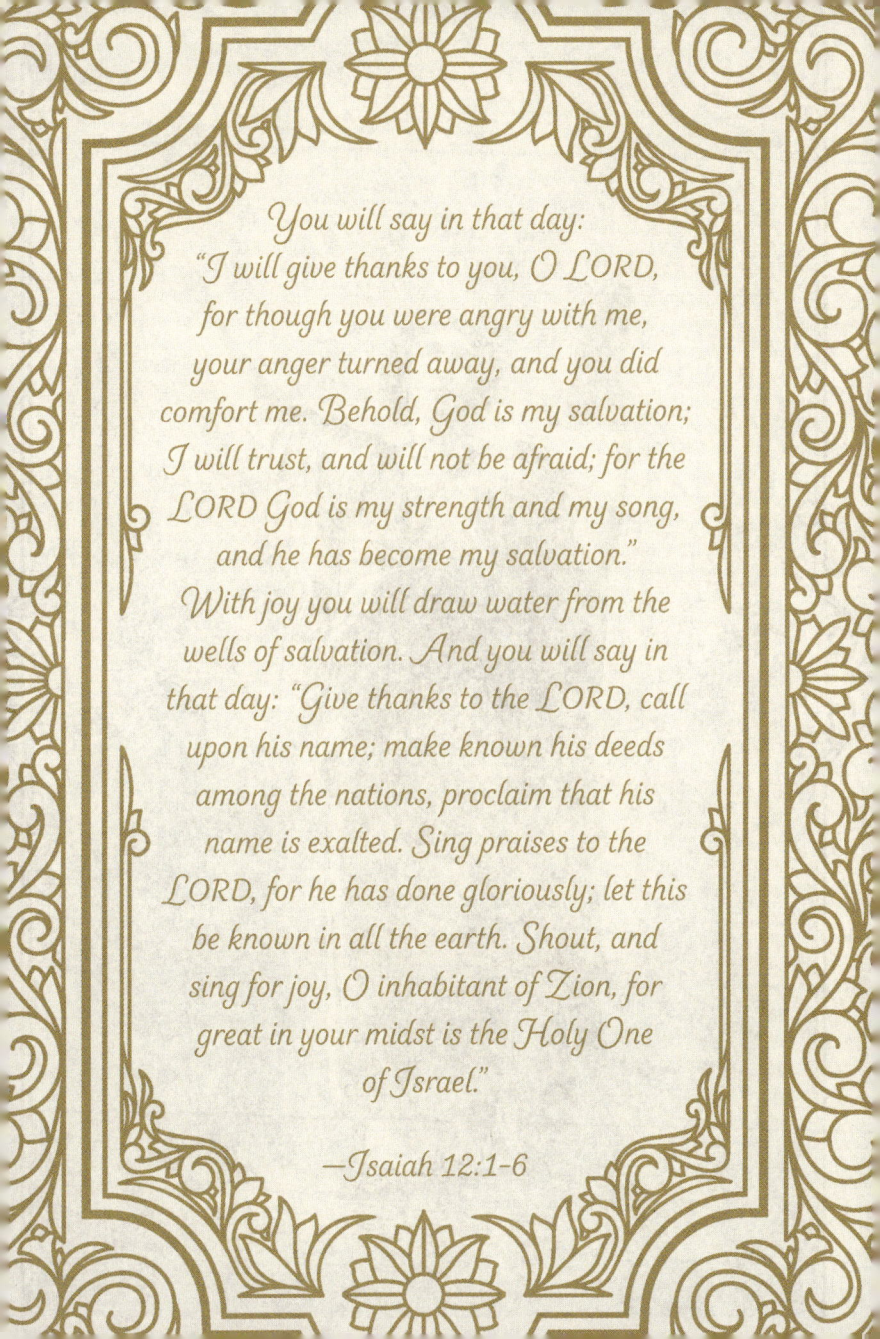

You will say in that day:
"I will give thanks to you, O LORD,
for though you were angry with me,
your anger turned away, and you did
comfort me. Behold, God is my salvation;
I will trust, and will not be afraid; for the
LORD God is my strength and my song,
and he has become my salvation."
With joy you will draw water from the
wells of salvation. And you will say in
that day: "Give thanks to the LORD, call
upon his name; make known his deeds
among the nations, proclaim that his
name is exalted. Sing praises to the
LORD, for he has done gloriously; let this
be known in all the earth. Shout, and
sing for joy, O inhabitant of Zion, for
great in your midst is the Holy One
of Israel."

—Isaiah 12:1-6

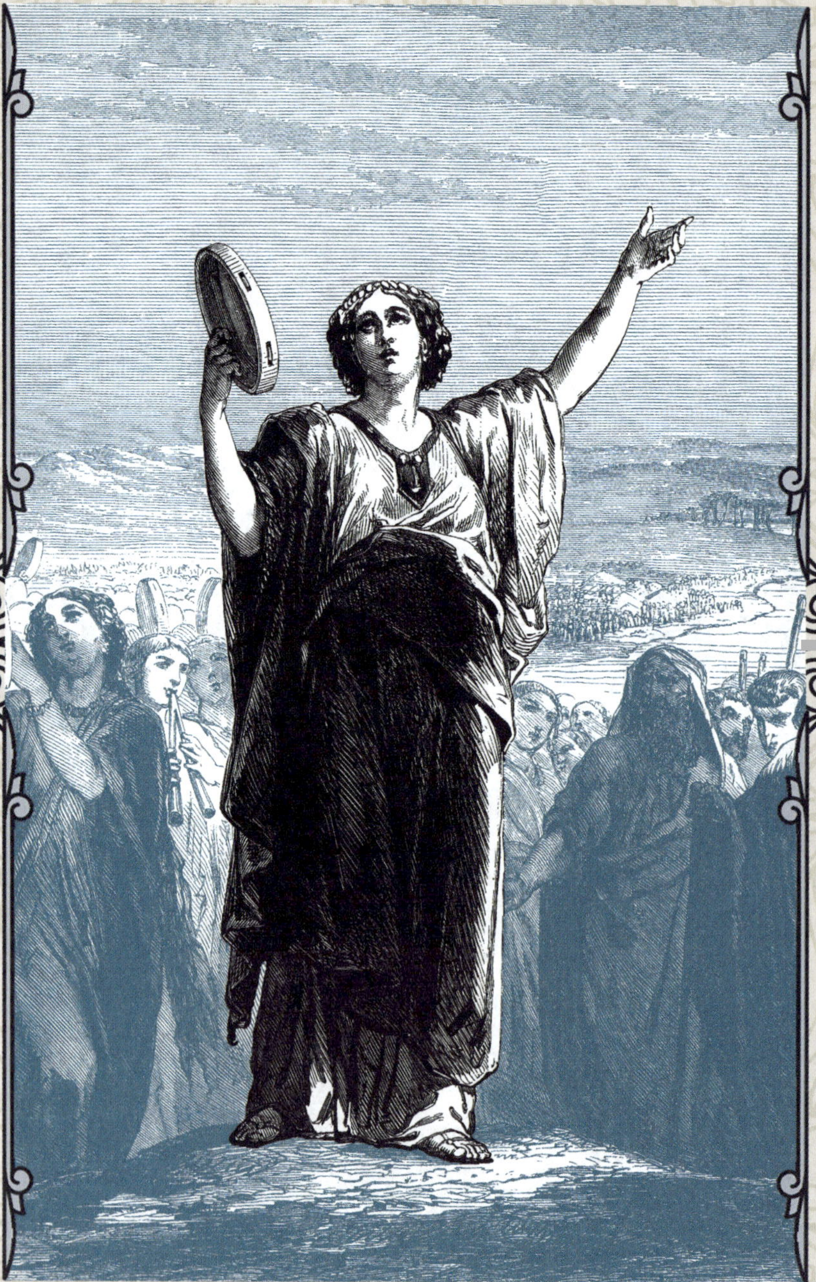

# Prayers of Thanksgiving and Praise

> Make a joyful noise to the LORD, all the lands! Serve the LORD with gladness! Come into his presence with singing! Know that the LORD is God! It is he that made us, and we are his; we are his people, and the sheep of his pasture. Enter his gates with thanksgiving, and his courts with praise! Give thanks to him, bless his name! For the LORD is good; his mercy endures for ever, and his faithfulness to all generations.
> —Psalm 100

| | | |
|---|---|---:|
| 147. | Act of Thanksgiving | 219 |
| 148. | Act of Adoration | 219 |

149. We Give Thanks to God—

    St. John Chrysostom                    220

150. For All the Times You Have Delivered Us—

    Servant of God Thea Bowman            220

## Act of Thanksgiving

O my God! I give thee thanks for having created me, for having preserved me, for having redeemed me by the blood of thy Son, for having made me a child of thy Church, and generally for all the favors I have received from thy infinite goodness.

## Act of Adoration

Great God! The Lord of heaven and earth! I prostrate myself before thee. With all the angels and saints, I adore thee. I acknowledge thee to be my Creator and sovereign Lord, my first beginning and last end. I render to thee the homage of my being and life. I submit myself to thy holy will; and I devote myself to thy divine service, now and forever.

## We Give Thanks to God

We give thanks to God that we have not sown our seed upon rocks, nor dropped it amid thorns; and that we have neither needed much time, nor long delay, in order that we might reap the harvest.

St. John Chrysostom

## For All the Times You Have Delivered Us

For all the times you have delivered us, O Lord, we give you thanks and praise. That you daily lead us from slavery into the freedom of the sons and daughters of God, O Lord, we give you thanks and praise. That you daily lead us toward the Land of Promise, O Lord, we give you thanks and praise. We sing and dance for joy, O Lord, we give you thanks and praise.

Servant of God Thea Bowman

# Acknowledgments

Acknowledgments are continued from the copyright page. Every effort has been made to properly acknowledge the sources of the prayers contained herein. When authorship is unknown, no attribution has been stated. Please inform the publisher of any omissions or amendments to these acknowledgments. Corrections will be made upon the next printing.

## *General Prayers*

The English translation of "Veni Sancte Spiritus (Come, Holy Spirit)" is reprinted from the *Lectionary for Mass*, copyright © 1997 International Commission on English in the Liturgy Corporation. Used by permission.

"Prayer to the Holy Family" by Pope Francis is reprinted from *Amoris Laetitia*, copyright © 2016 Libreria Editrice Vaticana. Used by permission.

## *Daily Prayers for Speaking with God throughout the Day*

"Lord, You Have Fed Us" is reprinted from the *Book of Blessings*, copyright © 1987 International Commission on English in the Liturgy, Inc. Used by permission.

The English translation of the "Suscipe Prayer" is reprinted from *Traditional Catholic Prayers*, edited by Msgr. Charles J. Dollen, copyright © 1990 by Our Sunday Visitor.

The English translation of "Actiones Nostras" is reprinted from the General Audience of April 35, 2012, given by Pope Benedict XVI, copyright © 2012 by Libreria Editrice Vaticana. Used by permission.

"Night Holds No Terrors for Me" is adapted from *The Liturgy of the Hours*, copyright © 1974 by the International Commission on English in the Liturgy, Inc. Used by permission.

"Protect Us, Lord" is adapted from *The Liturgy of the Hours*, copyright © 1974 by International Commission on English in the Liturgy Corporation. Used by permission.

## Prayers for the Sacrament of Reconciliation

"The Examination of Conscience Based on the Ten Commandments" copyright © 2013 United States Conference of Catholic Bishops. Used by permission.

"The Examination of Conscience Based on the Beatitudes" is reprinted from *Personal Encounter with Jesus Christ: The Sacrament of Reconciliation* copyright © 2020 Rosary Evangelization Apostolate. Used by permission.

## Prayers and Devotions to Jesus Christ

The English translation of "O Heart of Love" is reprinted from *Traditional Catholic Prayers*, edited by Msgr. Charles J. Dollen, copyright © 1990 by Our Sunday Visitor.

The English translation of the "Prayer before the Crucifix at San Damiano" by Francis of Assisi is reprinted from the General Audience of June 27, 2012, given by Pope Benedict XVI, copyright © 2012 by Libreria Editrice Vaticana. Used by permission.

## Prayers and Devotions to the Blessed Virgin Mary

The "Totus Tuus Prayer" and the "Act of Entrustment to Mary" by Pope John Paul II are used by permission of Libreria Editrice Vaticana.

"Prayer to Our Lady of Guadalupe, Patroness of the Americas" © 2012 United States Conference of Catholic Bishops. Used by permission.

"Prayer to St. Joseph, Man of Silence" is reprinted from the General Audience of December 15, 2021, given by Pope Francis, copyright © 2021 by Libreria Editrice Vaticana. Used by permission.

"St. Joseph, Just Man and Husband of Mary" is reprinted from the General Audience of December 1, 2021, given by Pope Francis, copyright © 2021 by Libreria Editrice Vaticana. Used by permission.

"St. Joseph, Father in Tenderness" is reprinted from the General Audience of January 19, 2022, given by Pope Francis, copyright © 2022 by Libreria Editrice Vaticana. Used by permission.

"Prayer to St. Joseph for the Protection of Workers" is reprinted from the General Audience of January 12, 2022, given by Pope Francis, copyright © 2022 by Libreria Editrice Vaticana. Used by permission.

## Prayers of Blessing

"Prayer of Blessing to Be Used in Various Circumstances," "Blessing of a Family, Blessing of a Married Couple," "Blessing of Children," "Blessing of a New Home," "Blessing of Homes during the Christmas and Easter Seasons," "Blessing on the Occasion of a Birthday," "Blessing on the Anniversary of a Baptism," "Blessing of an Engaged Couple," "Blessing of the Sick," "Blessing of a Person Suffering from Addiction," "Blessing of the Elderly," and "Blessing of Those Who Are Homebound" are reprinted from *Book of Blessings*, copyright © 1987 International Commission on English in the Liturgy, Inc. Used by permission.

"Godparent's Blessing of a Child" and "Prayer for the Dead" are reprinted from *Catholic Household Blessings and Prayers*, copyright © 1989 by the International Commission on English in the Liturgy, Inc. Used by permission.

"Prayer with the Dying" is adapted from "Prayer of Commendation" in *Catholic Household Blessings and Prayers*, copyright © 1989 by the International Commission on English in the Liturgy, Inc. Used by permission.

## Prayers for Special Graces

"The Litany of Trust" is written by the Sisters of Life (www.sistersoflife.org). Used by permission.

"Although My Frailty Is Great" and "Into Your Hands" are reprinted from *When God Is Silent* by Luis M. Martinez, copyright © 2014 by Sophia Institute Press. The book may be purchased at https://www.sophiainstitute.com/products/item/when-god-is-silent.

## Prayers of Surrender to God's Loving Will

Quotation from Chiara Badano is reprinted from "*In My Staying Is Your Going": The Life and Thoughts of Chiara Luce Badano*, copyright © 2021 by New City Press. Used by permission of the publisher.

## Prayers for the Grace of Forgiveness

"Prayer for Understanding" and "Prayer Asking for Mary's Help Forgiving Another" are adapted from the St. Josemaría Institute's "Novena for Forgiveness to St. Josemaría Escrivá." Used by permission of the Studium Foundation.

## Intercessory Prayers

The opening quotation from Bishop Ken Untener is used by permission of the Diocese of Saginaw.

"Prayer for Marriage and Families" by Pope John Paul II is used by permission of Libreria Editrice Vaticana.

"Families and Prayer for the Church through Mary's Intercession" is reprinted from the Homily of June 4, 1979, given by Pope John Paul II, copyright © 1979 by Libreria Editrice Vaticana. Used by permission.

"Prayer for Vocations" is reprinted from the Message of Pope Paul VI for the XV World Day of Prayer for Vocations, copyright © 1978 by Libreria Editrice Vaticana. Used by permission.

"Prayer for Priests" by Pope Benedict XVI is used by permission of Libreria Editrice Vaticana.

"Prayer for Peace" by Pope Francis © 2014 Libreria Editrice Vaticana. Used by permission.

"Prayer for Migrants and Refugees" is reprinted from the Message of His Holiness Pope Francis for the 108th World Day of

Migrants and Refugees © 2014 Libreria Editrice Vaticana. Used by permission.

"Prayer to Care for Our Common Home" by Pope Francis is reprinted from *Laudato Si'* © 2015 by Libreria Editrice Vaticana. Used by permission.

"Prayer for Community," "Prayer for Marginalized Persons," "Prayer for Healing for Victims of Abuse," and "Prayer for the Life and Dignity of the Human Person" are used by permission of the United States Conference of Catholic Bishops.

"Prayer for Priests through Mary's Intercession," attributed to Teresa of Calcutta, is used by permission of the Mother Teresa Center.

"Prayer for Our Country" by Theotonius Amal Ganguly is used by permission of the Congregation of Holy Cross.

"Prayer to Cooperate with the Holy Spirit's Movement in the World" and "Prayer for Breaking Racial and Social Barriers" by Thea Bowman are adapted from *Thea Bowman: In My Own Words* © 2009 by Maurice J. Nutt. Used by permission of Liguori Publications.

"Prayer to End Abortion" is used by permission of Priests for Life.

## Prayers of Thanksgiving and Praise

"For All the Times You Have Delivered Us" by Thea Bowman is adapted from *Thea Bowman: In My Own Words* © 2009 by Maurice J. Nutt. Used by permission of Liguori Publications.

# Index

Abba, Father, 155
abortion, end of, 210–211
abuse victims, 206–207
Act of Adoration, 219
Act of Charity, 17
Act of Consecration to the Sacred Heart of Jesus, 83–84
Act of Contrition I, 58
Act of Contrition II, 58
Act of Entrustment to Mary, 107–109
Act of Faith, 16
Act of Hope, 16
Act of Spiritual Communion, 15
Act of Thanksgiving, 219
Actiones Nostras, 38
addiction, 147
adoration, 71–76, 219
adults, birthday blessing, 143
afternoon prayer, 42

Alphonsus Liguori, St.
    Act of Spiritual Communion, 15
Although My Frailty is Great, 175
Andrè Bessette, St., xiii, 117, 129
Angel of God, 18
Angelus, 40–41
Anima Christi, 65
Anna Wang, St., 131
anniversaries
    baptism, 142
    birthdays, 143–144
    wedding, 136
Anselm, St., 165
Anthony of Padua, St.
    Behold the Cross of the Lord, 91
Apostles' Creed, 11

Augustine, St.
    God of Life, 158
    Watch, O Lord, 45
Ave Maris Stella, 101–102

baptism, 138, 139, 142
Beatitudes, Examination of Conscience Based on, 56–57
bedtime, 45–47
Behold the Cross of the Lord, 91
Benedict XVI, Pope
    Prayer for Priests, 196
Benedictus, 33–34
Bernard of Clairvaux, St.
    Memorare, 106
birthdays, 143–144
Bless Us, O Lord, 36
Blessed Sacrament
    adoration, 71–76
    Eucharist, 62–67
Blessing before Meals, 36
Blessing for the Special Occasions of Life, 134
Blessing of a Family, 135
Blessing of a Married Couple, 136–137
Blessing of a New Home, 140
Blessing of a Person Suffering from Addiction, 147
Blessing of an Engaged Couple, 145
Blessing of Children, 138–139
Blessing of Homes during the Christmas Season, 141
Blessing of Homes during the Easter Season, 141–142
Blessing of Manufactured Things, 133–134
Blessing of Natural Products, 133
Blessing of the Elderly, 148
Blessing of the Sick, 146
Blessing of Those Who Are Homebound, 149
Blessing on the Anniversary of a Baptism, 142
Blessing on the Occasion of a Birthday, 143–144
Bookmark of St. Teresa of Avila, 159
Bread of Heaven, 64
Bridget of Sweden, St., 115

Canticle of Mary, 43–44
Canticle of Simeon, 47
Canticle of Zechariah, 33–34
charity, 17

Chiara Badano, Bl., 77
    If You Want It, I Want It Too, 180
Chiara Corbella Petrillo, Servant of God
    Lord, Give Me the Grace to Welcome the Grace, 181
children
    baptized, 138
    birthdays, 143–144
    godparent's blessing of, 144
    not yet baptized, 139
Christ the King, Prayer to, 92
Christian unity, 192
Christmas season, 141–142
Clement of Rome, St.
    Grant Us Your Help and Protection, 190
Come, Holy Spirit, 9–10
communion, 62–67
community, 208
confidence, 174
Confiteor, 14
consecration, to the Sacred Heart of Jesus, 83–84
Constitutions of the Congregation of Holy Cross, xi

2 Corinthians
    **9:15**, 63
country and leaders, 199
couples
    engaged, 145
    married, 136–137
crucifix
    Behold the Cross of the Lord, 91
    prayer before, 90
    at San Damiano, prayer before, 91

daily prayers
    afternoon, 42
    bedtime, 45–47
    evening, 43–44
    midday, 40–41
    morning, 32–37
    before work, 38–39
Day in Your Courts Is Better Than a Thousand Elsewhere, A, 71
death and dying, 17, 150–151, 198
deliverance prayers, 162–163
dignity of the human person, 209–210
Divine Mercy Chaplet, 89
Divine Praises, 76

Dragon Is Here Again, The, 163

Easter season
    blessing of home, 141–142
    Regina Coeli, 41
elderly, 148, 149
Elizabeth Ann Seton, St., Prayer of, 156
engaged couples, 145
environment, 213–214
Eucharist, 62–67
Evening Prayer, 43–44
Examen, 46
Examination of Conscience
    based on the beatitudes, 56–57
    based on the ten commandments, 53–55
Exodus, Book of
    **3:4**, 71
Eyes of All Look to You, The, 36

faith, 16
families, 135, 191–192
For All the Times You Have Delivered Us, 220
forgiveness, 184–185

Frances Xavier Cabrini, St.
    Bread of Heaven, 64
Francis, Pope
    Prayer for Migrants and Refugees, 212
    Prayer for Peace, 200–201
    Prayer to Care for Our Common Home, 213–214
    Prayer to St. Joseph, Man of Silence, 123
    Prayer to St. Joseph for the Protection of Workers, 127
    Prayer to the Holy Family, 26
    St. Joseph, Father in Tenderness, 126
    St. Joseph, Just Man and Husband of Mary, 125
Francis of Assisi, St.
    Prayer before the Crucifix at San Damiano, 91
    Prayer of St. Francis, 39

Gautrelet, François-Xavier
    Morning Offering, 34
generosity, 181
Gertrude, St., 198

Glorious Mysteries, 114
Glory Be, 4
God of Life, 158
Godparent's Blessing of a Child, 144
Grace after Meals, 37
Grant Me the Favor I Implore, 155
Grant Us Your Help and Protection, 190
Gregory Nazianzus, St.
    The Dragon Is Here Again, 163

Hail Mary, 4
Have Mercy on Me, O God, 51
healing, 206–207
Hebrews, Book of
    **12**, xi
Henriette DeLille, Ven., 27
Here Am I, 71
Holy Family, 26
Holy Rosary, 113–114
Holy Spirit, 204
home
    blessing of a new, 140
    Christmas season blessing, 141
    Easter season blessing, 141–142
    homebound, 149
hope, 16
humility, 168–170

I Will Sing, 32
If You Want It, I Want It Too, 180
Ignatius of Loyola, St.
    Anima Christi, 65
    Prayer for Generosity, 181
    Suscipe Prayer, 35
illness, 146, 147, 149, 163
intercessory prayers
    for breaking racial and social barriers, 205
    to care for our common home, 213–214
    for Christian unity, 192
    for the Church through Mary, 193
    for community, 208
    for cooperation with the Holy Spirit's movement in the world, 204
    to end abortion, 210–211
    Grant Us Your Help and Protection, 190

for the life and dignity
of the human person,
209–210
for marginalized persons,
202–203
for marriage and
families, 191–192
for migrants and
refugees, 212
for our country, 199
for peace, 200–201
for priests, 196
for priests through Mary,
197–198
for seminarians, 195
for souls, 198
for victims of abuse,
206–207
for vocations, 194
Into Your Hands, 176
Isaiah, Book of
**12:1–6**, 215

Jesus Christ
Act of Consecration to
the Sacred Heart of
Jesus, 83–84
Behold the Cross of the
Lord, 91
Divine Mercy Chaplet,
89

Jesus Prayer, 5
Litany of the Sacred
Heart of Jesus, 85–88
O Heart of Love, 84
Prayer before a Crucifix,
90
Prayer before the
Crucifix at San
Damiano, 91
Prayer to Christ the
King, 92
St. Patrick's Breastplate,
81–82
Take My Heart, Dear
Lord, 82
Jesus Prayer, 5
John, Gospel of
**6:55–56**, 61
**19:27**, 107
John Berchmans, St., 1
John Bosco, St.
Prayer for Times of
Illness, 163
John Chrysostom, St.
We Give Thanks to God,
220
John Eudes, St.
Grant Me the Favor I
Implore, 155

John Paul II, St.
    Act of Entrustment to
        Mary, 107–109
    Prayer for Marriage and
        Families, 191–192
    Prayer for the Church
        through Mary's
        Intercession, 193
    *Rosarium Virginis Mariae*,
        113
    Totus Tuus Prayer, 110
John Vianney, St., 79
Josemaría Escrivá, St.
    Prayer Asking for
        Mary's Help Forgiving
        Another, 185
    Prayer for
        Understanding, 184
Joseph, St.
    Father in Tenderness,
        126
    Guardian of the Pure in
        Heart, 128
    Just Man and Husband
        of Mary, 125
    Litany of, 119–121
    Man of Silence, Prayer
        to, 123
    Memorare, 122
    Prayer to, for the
        Protection of Workers,
        127
    Prayer to Sleeping, 124
Josephine Bakhita, St., 29,
    153
Joyful Mysteries, 113
Julian of Norwich, St., 183
Julie Billiart, St.
    Act of Contrition II, 58
justice
    breaking racial and social
        barriers, 205
    community, 208
    cooperation with
        the Holy Spirit's
        movement in the
        world, 204
    end of abortion,
        210–211
    environmental, 213–214
    healing for victims of
        abuse, 206–207
    life and dignity of
        the human person,
        209–210
    marginalized persons,
        202–203
    for migrants and
        refugees, 212
    peace, 200–201

Index                    233

Lawrence, Br.
    Lord, I Cannot Do This Unless You Enable Me, 162
Litany of Humility, 168–170
Litany of Loreto, 103–106
Litany of Saints, 19–25
Litany of St. Joseph, 119–121
Litany of the Sacred Heart of Jesus, 85–88
Litany of Trust, 171–173
Lord, Give Me the Grace to Welcome the Grace, 181
Lord, I Cannot Do This Unless You Enable Me, 162
Lord, You Have Fed Us, 37
Lord's Prayer, 3
Loreto, Litany of, 103–106
Luis Maria Martinez, Servant of God, 161
    Although My Frailty is Great, 175
    Into Your Hands, 176
Luke, Gospel of
    **1:46–55**, 43–44
    **1:68–79**, 33–34
    **2:29–32**, 47
Luminous Mysteries, 114
Lutgarde of Aywieres, St.
    Take My Heart, Dear Lord, 82

Magnificat, 43–44
manufactured things, blessing of, 133–134
Margaret Mary Alacoque
    Act of Consecration to the Sacred Heart of Jesus, 83–84
    O Heart of Love, 84
Margaret of Cortona, St.
    This Morning My Soul Is Greater Than the World, 64
marginalized persons, 202–203
Marian prayers
    Act of Entrustment to Mary, 107–109
    Ave Maris Stella, 101–102
    Canticle of Mary, 43–44
    Holy Rosary, 113–114
    Litany of Loreto, 103–106
    Mary, I Love You, 97
    Memorare, 106
    Prayer for Asking Mary's Help Forgiving Another, 185
    Prayer for Priests through Mary's Intercession, 197–198

Prayer for the Church
through Mary's
Intercession, 193
Prayer to Our Lady of
Guadalupe, Patroness
of the Americas,
111–112
Stabat Mater, 98–100
Totus Tuus Prayer, 110
Mark, Gospel of
**10:21a**, 93
**14:36**, 155
married couples, 136–137,
191–192
Mary, I Love You, 97
Mass, Prayer before, 62–63
Matthew, Gospel of
**11:29–30**, 177
**26:39**, 179
mealtime prayers, 36–37
Memorare, 106
St. Joseph, 122
Merry del Val y Zulueta,
Rafael
Litany of Humility,
168–170
midday prayers, 40–41
migrants, 212
Morning Offering, 34
Morning Prayer, 33–34
morning prayers, 32–37

My Life Is an Instant, 35
Mysteries of Light, 114
Mysteries of the Holy Rosary,
113–114

natural products, blessing of,
133
Nicene Creed, 12–13
Niebuhr, Reinhold
Serenity Prayer, 167
Night Holds No Terrors for
Me, 45
Night Prayer, 47
Novena for Forgiveness,
184–185
Nunc Dimittis, 47

O Heart of Love, 84
O Jesus, I Surrender Myself
to You, 180
O Lord, You Have Searched,
59
O My Jesus Prayer, 5
O Salutaris Hostia, 73
O Saving Victim, 73
Our Father, 3
Our Lady of Guadalupe,
Prayer to, 111–112

Padre Pio, St.
    Prayer of Trust and Confidence, 174
Patrick, St.
    St. Patrick's Breastplate, 81–82
Paul VI, St.
    Prayer for Vocations, 194
peace, 200–201
penance
    Act of Contrition I, 58
    Act of Contrition II, 58
    Examination of Conscience Based on the Beatitudes, 56–57
    Examination of Conscience Based on the Ten Commandments, 53–55
    Have Mercy on Me, O God, 51
    O Lord, You Have Searched, 59
    Prayer before the Examination of Conscience, 51–52
    Prayer of Heartfelt Penitence and Thanksgiving, 59

petitionary prayers
    Abba, Father, 155
    Bookmark of St. Teresa of Avila, 159
    God of Life, 158
    Grant Me the Favor I Implore, 155
    Prayer of St. Elizabeth Ann Seton, 156
    Thank You, Lord Jesus Christ, 157
Philip Neri, St.
    Mary, I Love You, 97
Pia, Faustina Maria
    Litany of Trust, 171–173
Pierre Toussaint, Ven., 69
Prayer before a Crucifix, 90
Prayer before Mass, 62–63
Prayer before the Crucifix at San Damiano, 91
Prayer before the Examination of Conscience, 51–52
Prayer for Asking Mary's Help Forgiving Another, 185
Prayer for Breaking Racial and Social Barriers, 205
Prayer for Christian Unity, 192
Prayer for Community, 208

Prayer for Generosity, 181
Prayer for Healing for Victims of Abuse, 206–207
Prayer for Marginalized Persons, 202–203
Prayer for Marriage and Families, 191–192
Prayer for Migrants and Refugees, 212
Prayer for Our Country, 199
Prayer for Peace, 200–201
Prayer for Priests, 196
Prayer for Priests through Mary's Intercession, 197–198
Prayer for Seminarians, 195
Prayer for Souls, 198
Prayer for the Church through Mary's Intercession, 193
Prayer for the Dead, 151
Prayer for the Faithful Departed, 17
Prayer for the Life and Dignity of the Human Person, 209–210
Prayer for Times of Illness, 163
Prayer for Understanding, 184
Prayer for Vocations, 194

Prayer of Heartfelt Penitence and Thanksgiving, 59
Prayer of St. Elizabeth Ann Seton, 156
Prayer of St. Francis, 39
Prayer of Thanksgiving, 66–67
Prayer of Trust and Confidence, 174
Prayer to Care for Our Common Home, 213–214
Prayer to Christ the King, 92
Prayer to Cooperate with the Holy Spirit's Movement in the World, 204
Prayer to End Abortion, 210–211
Prayer to Our Lady of Guadalupe, Patroness of the Americas, 111–112
Prayer to Sleeping St. Joseph, 124
Prayer to St. Joseph, Man of Silence, 123
Prayer to St. Joseph for the Protection of Workers, 127
Prayer to the Holy Family, 26
Prayer with the Dying, 150
priests, 196, 197–198

Priests for Life
>Prayer to End Abortion, 210–211
Protect Us, Lord, 47
protection, 47, 190
Psalms, Book of
>**17:15**, 32
>**33:18–22**, 59
>**34:1–10**, vii
>**51:1–2, 10**, 51
>**59:16**, 32
>**84:10**, 71
>**100**, 217
>**139:1**, 59
>**145:15–16**, 36

Queen of Heaven, 41

racial barriers, 205
reconciliation
>Act of Contrition I, 58
>Act of Contrition II, 58
>Examination of Conscience Based on the Beatitudes, 56–57
>Examination of Conscience Based on the Ten Commandments, 53–55
>Have Mercy on Me, O God, 51
>O Lord, You Have Searched, 59
>Prayer before the Examination of Conscience, 51–52
>Prayer of Heartfelt Penitence and Thanksgiving, 59
refugees, 212
Regina Coeli, 41
Richard of Chichester, St.
>Thank You, Lord Jesus Christ, 157
Romans, Book of
>**8:26–27**, 49
*Rosarium Virginis Mariae* (John Paul II), 113
Ruotolo, Dolindo, 95
>O Jesus, I Surrender Myself to You, 180

sacraments
>baptism, 138, 139, 142
>Eucharist, 62–67
>reconciliation, 49–59
Sacred Heart of Jesus
>act of consecration to, 83–84
>litany of, 85–88

Saints, Litany of, 19–25
1 Samuel
    **3:9**, 72
seminarians, 195
Serenity Prayer, 167
sickness, 146, 147, 149, 163
Sign of the Cross, 3
social barriers, 205
Sorrowful Mysteries, 113
souls, 198
Speak, Lord, for Your Servant Hears, 72
special occasions, 134
    baptism anniversaries, 142
    birthdays, 143–144
    wedding anniversaries, 136
Spiritual Communion, Act of, 15
St. Joseph, Father in Tenderness, 126
St. Joseph, Guardian of the Pure in Heart, 128
St. Joseph, Just Man and Husband of Mary, 125
St. Joseph Memorare, 122
St. Michael the Archangel, 162
St. Patrick's Breastplate, 81–82

Stabat Mater, 98–100
strength, 175
surrender, 180–181
Suscipe Prayer, 35

Take My Heart, Dear Lord, 82
Tantum Ergo, 74–75
Te Deum, 6–8
Ten Commandments, Examination of Conscience Based on, 53–55
Teresa of Avila, St.
    Bookmark of, 159
Teresa of Calcutta, St.
    Prayer for Priests through Mary's Intercession, 197–198
Thanks Be to God, 63
thanksgiving, 59, 63, 66–67, 157, 219, 220
Thea Bowman, Servant of God
    For All the Times You Have Delivered Us, 220
    Prayer for Breaking Racial and Social Barriers, 205

Prayer to Cooperate
with the Holy Spirit's
Movement in the
World, 204
Theotonius Amal Ganguly,
Servant of God
Prayer for Our Country,
199
Thérèse of Lisieux, St., x
My Life Is an Instant, 35
Prayer for Seminarians,
195
Your Face Is the Only
Fatherland for Me, 72
This Morning My Soul Is
Greater Than the World,
64
Thomas Aquinas, St.
O Salutaris Hostia, 73
Prayer before Mass,
62–63
Prayer of Thanksgiving,
66–67
Tantum Ergo, 74–75
Three O'clock Prayer, 42
Totus Tuus Prayer, 110
trust, 171–173, 174

Untener, Ken, 187

Veni Sancte Spiritus, 9–10

vocations, 194

Watch, O Lord, 45
We Give Thanks to God, 220
wedding anniversaries, 136
When I Awake, 32
work and workers, 38–39,
127

Your Face Is the Only Fatherland for Me, 72

# Resources for Scripture Study and Prayer from Ave Maria Press

---

*The Ave Catholic Notetaking Bible (RSV2CE)*
Available in Hardcover and Imitation Leather

*The Ave Guide to Eucharistic Adoration*

*The Ave Guide to the Scriptural Rosary*

*The Ave Prayer Book for Catholic Mothers*

*The Ave Prayer Intentions Journal*

*Living the Word Catholic Women's Bible (RSV2CE)*
Available in Hardcover

*Living the Word Companion Journal*

Look for these titles wherever books and eBooks are sold.
Visit **avemariapress.com** to learn more.